Chief Engineer

Chief Engineer

LIFE OF A NATION BUILDER – SANDFORD FLEMING

LORNE GREEN

DUNDURN PRESS
Toronto & Oxford

Editor: Doris Cowan
Printed and bound in Canada by Gagné Printing Ltd., Louiseville, Quebec, Canada

The publisher wishes to acknowledge the generous assistance and ongoing support of **The Canada Council, The Book Publishing Industry Development Program** of the **Department of Communications, The Ontario Arts Council, The Ontario Publishing Centre** of the **Ministry of Culture, Tourism and Recreation,** and **The Ontario Heritage Foundation.**

Care has been taken to trace the ownership of copyright material used in the text. The author and publisher welcome any information enabling them to rectify any reference or credit in subsequent editions.

J. Kirk Howard, Publisher

Canadian Cataloguing in Publication Data

Green, Lorne Edmond.
    Chief Engineer : life of a nation builder – Sandford Fleming

Includes bibliographical references and index.
ISBN 1-55002-195-8

1. Fleming, Sandford, Sir, 1827–1915. 2. Railroad engineers – Canada – Biography.
I. Title.

HE2808.2.F54G7 1993   625.1'0092   C93-095352-5

Dundurn Press Limited	Dundurn Distribution	Dundurn Press Limited
2181 Queen Street East	73 Lime Walk	1823 Maryland Avenue
Suite 301	Headington, Oxford	P.O. Box 1000
Toronto, Canada	England	Niagara Falls, N.Y.
M4E 1E5	0X3 7AD	U.S.A. 14302-1000

Contents

CHAPTER 1

OLD AND NEW WORLDS

It is as hurtful to be condemned by neglect as by criticism; the inventor and adventurer Sandford Fleming suffered both in his lifetime, and he is for the most part little known today. To Fleming, of course, it makes no difference now, but we are the less for not knowing more about him, for even more important than Fleming's engineering triumphs is the witness of a remarkable life in contest with great natural and human adversities. Fleming laid the foundations of a railway across a continent; it was the most ambitious engineering project the world had yet known. He also strung a telegraph cable around the globe. But it is the quality of the man, how he confronted these and other daunting challenges, that has the power to speak to us. His was a life lived on a large playing field – a life of great achievement, but also one bedevilled by sinister forces and human failings.

Sandford Fleming was born to Andrew and Elizabeth Fleming in Kirkcaldy, Scotland, on 7 January 1827, a new life at the start of a new age, for the Industrial Revolution was gathering steam. Kirkcaldy's stern grey granite rows of high-roofed terrace houses, warehouses, and ship chandler shops follow the rock cliffs and sand shoreline on the north side of the Firth of Forth, almost directly opposite Edinburgh. The sweep of golden sand beach extends north to the ruins of the fifteenth-century Ravenscraig Castle; with its long seafront promenade the locals know Kirkcaldy as the "Lang Toun."

Fleming's Kirkcaldy was a firm beach-head of the Industrial Revolution. The introduction of cotton spinning brought two thousand weaving looms to the town, and created an unprecedented building boom; new buildings went up everywhere – banks, schools, churches, factories. Mostly, however, Kirkcaldy was a seaport. Local shipping on the Firth grew along with the economy; the product of the new industries was piled high on its quays, putting pressure on the dock and harbour works. It was a dour, honest, utilitarian town, the birthplace of Adam Smith and Robert Adam. Thomas Carlyle taught for a time at the Burgh School.

These were great times to be in the building trade; Sandford's father, Andrew, was one of Kirkcaldy's most successful building contractors. Andrew and Elizabeth, with their six sons and two daughters, lived in the considerable comfort of "Shirra Ha," a substantial, three-storey stone house set in gardens with a row of trees leading to the front door. A rabbit hutch stood in the garden; Andrew's building works and stabling for the cart horses were adjacent to the house. Shirra Ha was on Glasswork Street, just off the King's Gait, or High Street, running through the business district down to the seafront. The family lived in the commercial heart of the town.

The Industrial Revolution was good to Kirkcaldy, and to the Flemings. The development of the steam engine for transport had made the speedy movement of freight and large numbers of people possible for the first time. The world's first steam locomotion service, George Stephenson's Stockton and Darlington line, began two years before Fleming's birth. Coaches on earlier railway lines were towed along tracks by horses; Stephenson's innovation marked a quantum leap in transportation, even though in those early years there were persistent problems. The earliest, heavy locomotives were often more than the weak tracks could bear; sometimes frazzled railwaymen had to uncouple the steam engines from the coaches and resort to horsepower of the four-legged kind. Remarkably quick progress was made, however, and in 1830 the Liverpool and Manchester became the first public railway on which all traffic was hauled exclusively by steam locomotive. The enormous commercial potential of steam railway transport dawned and railway development took off; in 1843 Britain had 3,200 kilometres of railway line. By 1848 there were 8,000.

The young Sandford Fleming was closest to his brother David, two years older than himself. The boys climbed the hills of nearby Burntisland to shoot hares for supper; during school holidays they explored the wooded grounds of Raith Park, fished in its lake and picnicked by its waterfall. They rode in the back of their father's cart to their grandmother's house at Kennoway, a short distance along the coast. Sandford first attended school at Kennoway and later, as he advanced, his parents moved him to the Kirkcaldy Burgh School.

It was virtually preordained that Sandford Fleming, born into a builder's family in an age of feverish building activity, should be both practical and ambitious. He inherited his father's drafting and mechanical skills; Sandford excelled in mathematics at school, and his drawing attracted wide notice. A local printer was so impressed by Sandford's sketches of local attractions, such as Ravenscraig Castle and the castle standing in the middle of Loch Leven, that he struck a bargain with the boy to lithograph copies from his stonecuts.

Sandford's skill in mathematics and drawing also came to the notice of John Sang, one of Kirkcaldy's leading engineers and surveyors. Sang specialized in harbour works, waterworks, and railway surveys; he was engaged on the new railway lines from Edinburgh to Perth, and Perth to Dundee. Sandford Fleming, now fourteen years old, withdrew from school and became apprenticed to Sang, a stroke of extraordinary good luck to be associated with the nascent steam railway revolution.

For the next four years Fleming worked with Sang. He was at his workshop from eight-thirty in the morning until six at night, studying land measurements and calculations, mechanics, and astronomy, all under Sang's supervision; he also accompanied him on railway field work. At night Fleming worked by gaslight in his father's workshop, fashioning instruments, scales, compasses, and rulers from metal. The first stirrings of inventive genius were becoming apparent; Fleming devised a portrait machine to trace silhouettes from life models onto a paper backdrop; his parents sat dutifully while Sandford manipulated the contraption to trace the outline of their profiles. Fleming's pastimes reflected his mathematical skills. He was an avid chess player and regular contender for the Kirkcaldy chess club championship title (the "Caliphate"). The club executive also enlisted Sandford's talents to draft a new paper chessboard for the members' use.

No chess was played in the Fleming house on Sunday; the strict religious devotion of a Scottish Presbyterian family would not permit it. Instead, the Fleming family, all ten of them, filled a church pew at least twice, and often three times, each Sunday without fail. Sandford's travels in later life often took him far from a church building, but he never deviated from regular Sunday worship wherever he found himself.

The pace of economic life in nineteenth-century Britain grew with lightning speed, but not everyone benefited equally. There was no comprehensive regime of labour laws to regulate terms and conditions of employment; merciless landlords in Scotland forced tenants from the land and replaced them with sheep. The disillusioned and the displaced looked beyond, many to the frontiers of North America with their promise of abundant land free for the working, and freedom from the rapaciousness of factory managers and landlords. Every family in Kirkcaldy would have known someone who emigrated, and most of the reports sent back from the New World were overwhelmingly positive. Sandford's Kennoway schoolmaster went to Canada, as did one of his father's workmen. A more significant influence was John Hutchison, a cousin of Sandford's father; he was a medical doctor who had emigrated to Canada, and on a return visit to Kirkcaldy in 1842 told enticing stories of the adventure of pioneer life in the promising new settlements of British North America. Andrew Fleming was smitten; he had profited well from Kirkcaldy's building boom, but he had the future of eight children to think about. While there was no doubt in his mind that prospects were better in Canada, a streak of Scottish common sense in him counselled caution;

Andrew Fleming wrote to his cousin in Peterborough, Canada, in July 1844:

> I would have sent out David my oldest son but cannot well
> spare him as he is now taking the management of the work
> shop … If Mr. Sang does not get busy we have made up our
> minds to send Sandford although we have doubts of him
> getting any employment in his profession. Still he will have
> some chance; he will not lose much even although he should
> have to return to the land of his fathers. I still think were we
> all to be landed safe in your neighbourhood … we have lit-
> tle to fear.[1]

By the beginning of 1845 it was agreed in the Fleming household that both David and Sandford should try their luck in Canada. Dr. Hutchison would be there to help them make a start, and if things went well for them the rest of the family would follow. Andrew Fleming and Sandford journeyed up to Balbirnie to call on the prominent Aberdeen native and member of Parliament Edward Ellice, to enquire about the prospect of the boys going out to Canada. Ellice had large fur trade and land interests in British America, and was very well connected; he obliged them with letters of introduction.

The transatlantic shipping season resumed in mid-April after the winter. Family and friends gathered at Shirra Ha on the eve of their departure to wish them well, and the following morning David and Sandford were up at six to finish packing the iron-clad leather sea trunks and loading them on the cart, which then conveyed both luggage and boys down Glasswork Street to the docks, and the waiting Edinburgh steamer. Their brothers and sisters raced along the beach, waving handkerchiefs in the air as the steamboat slipped away from the quay. Andrew Fleming accompanied his two sons to Edinburgh, then to Glasgow by train. They booked on the sailing ship *Brilliant* for £13 10s. each. Water and provisions, fires and suitable berths were supplied by the ship; utensils and bedding were the responsibility of the passengers. The two days remaining to the Flemings were taken up with buying and packing supplies for the long ocean crossing ahead.

The *Brilliant* cleared the wharf at one-thirty on a fine April afternoon, and was towed by a steamer down the Clyde to the open sea. As Glasgow receded from view, David and Sandford could see Andrew, at the end of the wharf, giving his sons three cheers. They wondered – as he must also have done – whether he would ever see them again. Sandford's journal of the voyage is a marvellous account of an experience undergone by millions of migrants from the Old World to the New.

Passengers began to succumb to sea sickness as soon as the *Brilliant* reached the open sea. Two days out Sandford was stricken as they ran into heavy seas. Passengers and crew busied themselves with wedging the trunks into place in the hold, and lashing them down to prevent shifting as the ship pitched. Pots and pans began to slide from one side of the cabin to the other, "A frying pan which hung to the roof amongst the tin things fell during the night on a large jar of treacle and broke it all to pieces; the floor was swimming with treacle which made it more difficult to walk on, when the ship was rocky."* The deck was soon awash with broken bottles, eggs, and cakes; the passengers slipped and fell in the mess, and without proper laundry facilities their clothes got into a terrible state.

A week out of Glasgow, the sea's fury struck with a vengeance; Sandford and David had to struggle not to be pitched from their beds. Even the pillows were lashed down:

> As the evening advanced the storm grew worse. The sea sometimes washed across the deck. I never expected to see daylight again, when a great wave swept above our heads. It had a sound as if the sea was closing over us. We slept none all night, the timbers were cracking terribly, the bottles and tins rattling from one side of the floor to the other — pity the poor sailors on deck all night.

There were moments of laughter, too, in the midst of the peril.

> The weight of the boxes burst the nails that nailed them to the floor, they all slid to the opposite side of the cabin, some on their sides and others on their tops; they came back with the ship and went smashing to and fro, with us holding on and laughing at the sport and others sitting on the tops of the boxes. The scene which ensued was laughable enough and can scarcely be described. David had been sitting on the box containing 2 doz. port, 2 doz. ale and 2 bottles whisky, 2 bottles pickles; his feet and legs were wet with port etc. and the floor was swimming, the laughing was abundant. Here is the charm of emigration; again they cross the floor, one huge trunk came smash on the ladder, breaking one of the feet and down it came crash among the pots and tins that are dancing all through the floor. We were surprised to pick out 2½ doz. whole bottles which the straw had saved; they were handed one by one into the beds as they were picked from amongst the rubbish.

---

*This and subsequent direct quotes from Fleming are taken from his travel journal and diaries now held in the National Archives of Canada, Sandford Fleming Papers.

The storm continued unabated; by the beginning of May it was doubtful the ship could ride it out. Despairing of their fate Sandford sealed a letter to his father and tossed it into the sea. Amazingly, seven months later, and well after the boys had landed safely in Canada, their father received the following note from Devonshire:

> Sir, a bottle has been drifted on shore here this day and been picked up by a poor fisherman. It contains a letter written by Sandford Fleming and is addressed to his father. It bears date – Atlantic Ocean 1st May and excites great curiosity having drifted about 630 miles. The letter may be of consequence and it should be preserved for the owner.

The weather cleared at the end of the second week, and the passengers could at last find their sea-legs and begin to enjoy the voyage. Sandford and David made friends with the young crewmen who lent them Atlantic charts and navigation books so that they could follow the ship's progress. In the evening there was singing in the steerage, with everyone joining in, and sometimes dancing on the deck to the music of David's flute. Sandford filled his sketchbook with drawings of the sailors and passing ships. The boys played chess, and when the weather was fine they watched for porpoises, whales, and seabirds.

The rudimentary laundry and cooking facilities were on deck; passengers took turns getting up at 4:30 a.m. to light the fire for breakfast – no easy thing to do with constant sea spray washing across the deck. For breakfast they ate porridge and treacle, for lunch perhaps some red herrings or pancakes, beef and broth or potato soup in the evening, and figs, or scones and jam, for dessert.

Land was sighted on 22 May:

> I was just appearing on deck to put out some handkerchiefs to dry, when agreeably surprised I was to see hills on the horizon; they had been hid by the mist. Immediately everyone came on deck, some nearly dancing for joy; I took a sketch as it there appeared. This was the south coast of Newfoundland, the first I have seen of the New World, the first of our adopted country.

Two weeks later, on 5 June, the *Brilliant* sailed into the harbour at Quebec City, the rising sun glinting on the tin roofs and spires of the town.

The St. Lawrence River was crowded with sailing ships loading timber for England, with pilot boats darting about in every direction. Hitching a ride ashore on a pilot boat, Sandford and David to their amazement beheld a scene of great desolation.

> Very happy to get our feet on terra firma once more, we set off to see the ruins of a great fire which had taken place one or two days before. It had an awful appearance – more than 20 acres of houses were burnt to the ground, nothing left but a forest of blackened chimneys, the houses being chiefly built of wood, the pavement of the streets being made of wood was also burnt. It was really a melancholy catastrophe. The inhabitants thus made homeless were lodged in churches and other large buildings and subscriptions were raised in every quarter for their support.

A devastating fire had swept Quebec City on 28 May leaving one hundred dead and sixteen thousand homeless in its wake. In a stroke of cruel irony exactly one month later, on 28 June, a second fire claimed the houses of thousands more.

Most of the *Brilliant's* passengers transferred to the westbound mail coach from Quebec, but Sandford and David boarded a paddle-wheel steamer making its maiden voyage to Montreal. The St. Lawrence for three kilometres above Quebec was congested with a forest of sailing vessels taking on cargoes of wood. The steamer's side paddles were too wide for the river locks and it became stuck at the first barrier; the paddle boxes were removed to haul the vessel through, a process repeated at various stages along the river to Montreal. The novel sights of the Canadian frontier compensated the boys for their painfully slow progress.

> I have never forgotten seeing a settler frying bacon in a pan whose handle was as long as a broom-stick. This was a striking example of adapting familiar things to the peculiarities of a new life. The short-handled frying pan would have been quite useless in connection with a large campfire.

Montreal presented a spectacle entirely unlike the charred ruins of Quebec City; the establishment of the seat of government here had spurred Montreal's development. The narrow old streets were congested with commerce; merchants lived over their warehouses. The old town was entirely built up and it was only on streets like St. James, Craig, and McGill that there were gaps. The few residences above St. Catherine Street stood like manor houses in the fields that extended down to Dorchester Street. Montreal was the headquarters for the western fur trade, and was developing an important retail trade; it garrisoned a large contingent of British troops who paraded in the Champ de Mars. The population numbered about 60,000. By great coincidence, Sandford and David ran into the Kennoway schoolmaster who had emigrated several years before to become master of the Montreal High School.

At Montreal the boys boarded a river barge, one of several hauled in tandem by a towboat; the boat-train moved slowly up to the Ottawa River, ever deeper into the Canadian hinterland, and through the Carillon Canal on its way to Bytown. The string of barges was so crowded that it became stuck in the mud just below Lachine, and Sandford and David spent the night there on deck, under an oilskin to keep out the pelting rain. They were moving again next morning but progress was slow; pausing at the river locks, they went ashore for fresh milk and food from the farms along the shore. On June 14, the string of barges passed the Rideau Falls and its mill, where the Rideau River spills into the Ottawa, rounded Nepean Point and drew into the wharf at Bytown. It was hardly imaginable that this lumber town was destined to become Canada's capital. Just above the dock were the newly opened locks leading to the Rideau Canal spanned by the Sappers' Bridge; public buildings stood among the trees on either side of the canal, army barracks and hospital high on a bluff of land overlooking the river where one day Canada's Parliament Buildings would stand. In Bytown the boys met their father's former workman, who had left Kennoway eleven years before.

Continuing on their slow progress, the string of barges passed through the Rideau Lakes to Kingston on Lake Ontario, another Canadian community in the making:

> A pretty considerable town – wide streets and well laid out. There are some good public buildings – most especially the Market House which is extensive and splendid, in the form of T with colonnade and pillars in front supporting a door and clock tower, with the roof covered in tin. There are some good churches, a new gothic structure, and a large, plain college.

Queen's College had opened a few years earlier and would figure large in Fleming's later life.

At Kingston, the boys transferred to a crowded steamer packed with Irishmen bound for Toronto, but they left it at Cobourg where they hitched a ride with a farmer who took them on the last leg of their journey to Peterborough, then a little town of scarcely two thousand people. They rumbled along the rough corduroy road, and ten weeks from Scotland, and eleven days from Quebec, Sandford and his brother arrived at the front door of their father's cousin, Dr. John Hutchison. The doctor had one of the most substantial houses in Peterborough, which was still little more than a frontier settlement, with stumps of trees in the middle of the streets, a wood house here and there, and a few better villas. Hutchison was one of the town's first settlers and most prominent citizens.

It is inconceivable by modern standards of travel for a journey from Glasgow to the heart of Canada to take ten weeks, but in the last century it was typical, and quite acceptable. The days of ocean steamship travel were only beginning when Sandford and David crossed the Atlantic; it was still an expensive luxury that they could not afford. The river steamers that plied the St. Lawrence and the Great Lakes were uncomfortable and slow, but they were a tremendous improvement over the poor roads – rough and dusty in summer, a sea of mud in spring and fall, and impassable in winter except by sleigh – despite the fact that the winter freeze-up of Canada's waterways also reduced water traffic to a crawl for nearly half the year. In due course steam railway development would revolutionize transport in British America as it was doing in Britain, and accelerate development of the new frontier.

David found employment much more easily than Sandford did; a trained carpenter in his father's workshop, he soon secured a position with a Toronto cabinetmaker. Since there were no opportunities for an apprentice engineer in Peterborough, Sandford too went to Toronto, carrying letters of introduction from the Aberdeen member of Parliament, Edward Ellice, to two of Toronto's most influential citizens, Bishop Strachan and Casimir Gzowski, either of whom could open almost any door in the Province of Canada. Strachan had founded King's College, later secularized to become the University of Toronto; Gzowski, a brilliant Polish engineer, was in charge of the Department of Roads and Harbours. Both men received the young Fleming but neither encouraged him; Gzowski was particularly gloomy. As Sandford wrote:

> Called again at Mr. Gzowski's ... he knew nothing in the province; the great works were nearly finished and the funds were exhausted and they would require to pay off several of the assistants in a short time. In fact he thought it a very bad country for professional men and would advise me as the most profitable for myself to return to Scotland.

This was just plain bad advice. A Toronto architect acquaintance told Fleming not to be put off by Gzowski, who wanted to monopolize Canada's engineering works and frighten all young upstarts out of the country.

Fleming had too much riding on his success in Canada to turn back; his family in Scotland were counting on him and David to prepare the way for their emigration. He did not seriously consider returning, in spite of letters from home telling him that surveyors were in great demand in Scotland. Sandford's father, Andrew, wrote to his cousin, John Hutchison, in Peterborough, "I hope that Sandford will get something to do, if not as surveyor or engineer, he must work with his hands, or try and teach mathematics or some one thing or other not to be idle." For Andrew's part the implications of uprooting his family, leaving his business behind, and emigrating weighed heavily on him; he confided to Hutchison:

> I do not know how to act. Several families depend in great measure upon me. Had I none but myself and family I would soon break off although I will have ill getting hold of the needful, property has fallen greatly in Kirkcaldy. I believe what I have will be from one to two thousand pounds less.[2]

Sandford, meanwhile, carried his job search from Toronto to Hamilton, Guelph, and Port Dover, and then back again. His money was running low. He sought out architects in particular, showing them his sketches of the countryside and local churches in hopes that his drawing skills would be recognized. In the end it was a word from Dr. Hutchison to a government surveyor that got him a position as journeyman surveyor.

While boarding with the Hutchisons, Sandford continued with his sketches. One of them, a detailed drawing of the Peterborough court house and the local church, attracted the attention of the priest who called round to ask him to make the working plans and specifications for finishing the Catholic Church. He also made friends: there were quite a number of young people of his age in Peterborough and the tall, gangly young Scotsman, his large head framed by his reddish hair, became a familiar figure at social gatherings. Sheriff Hall's daughter, who lived down the hill from Dr. Hutchison, made a particularly deep impression on him. A decade later, Jeanie Hall would become a permanent part of Sandford's life.

In the first half of 1846 Fleming prepared a complete survey of Peterborough, including house plans and surveyed lots. He placed notices around town advertising copies for sale, and the initial forty-five copies were soon sold out. Fleming then transferred the plan to stone and printed a further 235 copies – they became some of the finest earliest examples of lithography in Canada. A sketch of Toronto Cathedral was similarly printed in number. Buoyed by the popular success of these first ventures, Fleming undertook a plan of Cobourg and Newcastle District; the map he produced is regarded as the first accurately surveyed large-scale rural map produced in Canada. A Toronto engraving firm, Scobie and Balfour, took on Fleming to produce lithographs of his map but the bench work was tedious to him. He was much happier carrying copies of his prints about the countryside in search of buyers.

Now that David and Sandford had found their feet, Andrew Fleming concluded that the time had arrived for the rest of the family to make their move. He wrote to the boys in Canada, "You can be looking about you and gather all the information you can regarding business and trades, and how they remunerate, or whether they require much capital to commence and carry on, as also the risk of making bad debts or losses etc. and whether suited to a larger or smaller town or the country."

The entire family arrived in Canada in 1847, settling on the Humber River near Toronto. Andrew Fleming bought a saw mill; Sandford and David spent the summer helping their father put the mill in working order, cutting lumber, erecting fences and laying out a garden.

Sandford secured a position with a Weston surveyor, J. Stoughton Dennis, in spring 1848 and set about seriously to train for a government commission as a full-fledged provincial land surveyor. Dennis was engaged at the time on a survey of Toronto, more ambitious by far than Fleming's surveys of Peterborough and Cobourg; the survey team was based at Upper Canada College. Fleming found the premises, with its windows too high to see out, an exceedingly dull workplace, but here he toiled with a fellow apprentice, Charles Unwin, who later would become chief surveyor of Toronto. Fleming and Unwin began the enormous job of reducing the city plan of Toronto to scale, with Fleming doing the engraving. The better part of the work was in the field, measuring streets and surveying building lots. By this time Fleming had lived in various Toronto digs, boarding houses first, then a house bought by his father at the corner of Richmond and Victoria streets. Along with his work for Dennis, Fleming still did the occasional engraving job for Scobie and Balfour, and continued to sell copies of his various maps.

Fleming's work on the Toronto survey carried his thoughts to other aspects of town planning; one of his most imaginative was a novel plan for street lighting:

I have been thinking for some time that the charcoal lights of the magnetic battery might be brought to some practical use. I only require one experiment, but it would be an expensive one for me unless I could meet with a powerful battery, but I don't think there is one in Canada. It is to try if more than one light can be formed with one set of wires by breaking the connection and interposing charcoal points. If this is the case we have a good and cheap substitute for gas, would give a much better light and at least could be easily adapted to lighting streets or churches just by having a wire like telegraph ones with a charcoal appliance here and there. Worth trying.

The apprentice surveyor spent many evenings at the Mechanics Institute, which was frequented by Toronto's engineering community, to attend lectures and take geometry classes in preparation for the provincial land surveyor examination. He brought a model locomotive before the institute's committee on railways to perform an experiment intended to show the merits of the steam railway system, in the face of considerable scepticism about this costly new mode of transport. In 1849, a year after beginning work on the Toronto survey, Sandford was ready to sit for the exams at the Crown Land Office in Montreal. Once river navigation opened for the season he was on his way.

Montreal, the capital of the Province of Canada, was seething with trouble when Fleming arrived; he saw an angry mob congregate on the Champ de Mars on 25 April, run riot, storm the Parliament Building and set it alight.

This is a memorable day. The Governor, Lord Elgin, gave his assent to the Rebellion Losses Bill, which not excluding rebels from receiving pay for loss sustained in 1837 gives a great deal of dissatisfaction. The Governor was pelted with eggs when coming out, the windows of Parliament House were smashed by the mob and lastly the building set alight – very little was saved.

Fleming rushed into the blazing building in a vain attempt to save some of the rare books he had seen earlier that day in the Parliamentary Library; but thrown back by the flames, he entered the legislative council chamber and, with three other men, rescued the portrait of Queen Victoria from its place over the Speaker's chair. Next morning the Montreal *Gazette* reported that four scoundrels had been seen carrying off the portrait.

Excitement apart, Fleming did pass his exams, and the governor signed the licence confirming him as a provincial land surveyor.

In June, Fleming met with a group of ten surveyors and engineers in the office of the Toronto architect Kivas Tully, to discuss the setting up of a "Canadian Institute" to promote scientific knowledge and research. They sent a prospectus to five hundred people throughout the province; twelve replied. So the institute got off to a shaky start, and went down hill from there. At its lowest point, the February 1850 meeting, only two members, Fleming and F.F. Passmore, showed up. They were determined, however, not to let the institute die; they constituted themselves a quorum and decided that henceforth it would meet weekly, and that the first subject for discussion be the act for regulating the admission of land surveyors and the survey of lands throughout the province. The membership climbed back up and the institute went from strength to strength, meeting weekly to hear papers presented by the members. As the group broadened its appeal it united with the Toronto Athenaeum in 1855 and thereby fell heir to a library; thirty years later the Natural History Society amalgamated with it, and in due course it was granted a royal charter to become known henceforth as the Royal Canadian Institute. Fleming was a frequent contributor to the institute's proceedings all his life, with papers on all manner of subjects from the improvement of Toronto Harbour to the design of postage stamps.

Licensed now as a provincial land surveyor, Fleming rented a second-floor office over the Bentley Drug Store on Yonge Street, Toronto. Once the Toronto city plan was published in 1851, Fleming turned his attention to the mapping of Toronto Harbour and adjacent shoreline of Lake Ontario. Day after day he went out in a rowboat to take soundings of the harbour bottom and make measurements with a cleverly devised floating wood chain. The resultant Toronto Harbour study, again engraved by Fleming, stood as the definitive work of its kind for many years. Its quality established Fleming as an accomplished nautical surveyor and led to him being engaged that same year to produce a plan of York, Scarborough, and Pickering lakeshore for a planned terminus at Port McNicholl. Fleming was also engaged on a survey of a projected Toronto-to-Kingston railway line. During this period he worked on several Toronto improvements including the preservation of the harbour esplanade and waterfront, and together with Kivas Tully the designs for Trinity College.

The provincial agricultural fair returned to Toronto in 1852 after several years' absence. It was decided to build a permanent hall to house the fair, the promoters likely inspired by the success of the Crystal Palace at the London Exhibition in 1851. A competition for designs was announced in which the speed of construction and economy were critical factors. Fleming, with a partner, Collingwood Schreiber, decided to enter the competition. Schreiber was an English engineer who had arrived in Canada in 1852. He was to work with Fleming most of his life.

Fleming and Schreiber's design won the competition: it was a cruciform structure of cast iron and glass to be known as the Palace of Industry. The Palace was erected from prefabricated sections in three months and opened officially by the governor general of Upper Canada, Sir Edmund Walker, in September 1858.

Fleming was now, at the age of twenty-seven, part of Toronto's engineering establishment; in 1854 he was appointed to the board of examiners for the Upper Canada provincial land surveyor's licence. Of course he was also a recognized designer and lithographer, and it was on this basis that Canada's first postmaster general, James Morris, approached Fleming for help in the conception of Canada's first postage stamps. After some initial rejections Fleming came up with an agreed design – the three-penny beaver, which became Canada's first adhesive postage stamp and was issued for public use in April 1851. The choice of the beaver was inspired since on the one hand it symbolized industriousness and on the other the fur trade, which had been such a large part of Canada's foundation. Fleming also designed the six-penny Prince Albert and the twelve-penny Queen Victoria. At first they were issued in unperforated sheets of a hundred; five years later, perforated sheets appeared. Fleming was establishing Canadian institutions. He was also becoming something of one himself.

CHAPTER 2

ON THE RAILS

A spectacular parade wound through the city of Toronto on 15 October 1851, and there was a grand ball in the evening with the "Swedish nightingale," Jenny Lind, in attendance. The festivities were all in celebration of the turning of the first sod to begin construction of the Ontario, Simcoe and Huron Railway. That ceremony was performed, with a silver spade, by the governor general's wife, Lady Elgin. Fleming took home with him the historic sod dug up by Lady Elgin's spade; here, after all, was history in the making.

Steam locomotion was still very much a novelty in British America. Steam had first been used on Canadian soil in 1830 to power the cable cars carrying building materials up the steep slope from the river shore of Quebec City for the construction of the Citadel. Six years later, in July 1836, the Champlain and St. Lawrence, running 23.2 kilometres from the south shore of the St. Lawrence to St. John's on the Richelieu River, became Canada's first steam railway line, and remained the only public line in the Province of Canada up to 1847. In that year 68.8 kilometres of line were completed. The total distance increased to 106.6 kilometres in 1850; 35.2 were added the following year and a further 190.4 in 1852.

The chief engineer of the Ontario, Simcoe and Huron, Frederick Cumberland, took Fleming on as assistant engineer in 1852. Fleming, Cumberland, and another assistant, Alfred Brunel (brother of the famous English engineer) tramped the rugged country from Barrie to Georgian Bay, plotting the route for the railway line through a tangle of brush, dense forest, rock and swamps. One hot dry summer day, Fleming and Cumberland stopped at a farm house to ask for a drink of milk. They were shown into the parlour, its curtains drawn to keep out the sun; the farmer's wife brought in a jug of milk and poured out two tall glasses. The two men gulped down their drink avidly until Cumberland heard a clinking sound at the bottom of his glass; he carried it over to the window and drew the curtain back for a closer look. He beat a hasty retreat from the house when he saw the foreign object in the glass – the old lady had poured the milk into the glass holding her best set of false teeth!

The engineers chose a desolate stretch of swamp on Georgian Bay for the northern terminus of the railway, a site known as "Hen and Chickens" for the string of islands off-shore, but later renamed Collingwood. Fleming later bought a parcel of fertile land near Collingwood for his father to clear and establish a farm there.

The first section of the Ontario, Simcoe and Huron opened between Toronto and Aurora in May 1853, and two years later the first train travelled all the way from Toronto to Collingwood. The line chiefly carried lumber and firewood south from the dense cedar forests along Georgian Bay.

Fleming had other things on his mind as well. Jeanie Hall had remained his friend since they first met in Peterborough when Sandford arrived in 1845. Jeanie was both amiable and refined; Fleming was smitten. Their attachment deepened during a romantic but perilous episode: they were travelling from Toronto to Peterborough in January 1854 when the sleigh overturned and the horses ran away. Thrown to the ground, Fleming struck his head on a tree stump and lay unconscious in the snow. Jeanie escaped serious injury and managed to get him to a farmhouse where she nursed him until he was well enough to carry on to Peterborough. A year later they were married. Sandford and his bride returned to Toronto by horse and wagon over the very road where they had almost met their doom; Fleming brought the wagon to a stop by the tree stump on which he had hit his head, chopped it out of the ground and later made a cradle from the wood in readiness for the first baby. Years later he presented Jeanie with a photograph of their children in a frame made from the stump.

Sandford and Jeanie settled in a small house on Carlton Street, Toronto. Shortly after his marriage Fleming succeeded Cumberland as chief engineer of the Ontario, Simcoe and Huron, now renamed the Northern Railway; Brunel became superintendent. The line got off to a shaky start; mistakes were made in its operation – unrealistic low prices were quoted for cargo contracts to attract business, the Canadian-made locomotives were found wanting and the rails began to deteriorate almost as fast as they were laid. The line was not fenced, so farmers' livestock roamed at will on to the tracks; on one typical day the train struck three cows and left the track. In time, however, problems were ironed out and traffic and profits increased.

When Sandford was not in the field he and Jeanie travelled back and forth to the Fleming family farm, Craigleith, near Collingwood, and to Peterborough to visit Jeanie's parents. Their first son, Franky, was born in 1855, followed by a second, Sandford Hall (known as "Bobby"), two years later. They were followed in turn by two girls, Minnie in 1859 and Lily in 1861. Two other children died in infancy.

The outbreak of civil war in the United States led to a great deal of unsettlement in the British American colonies; Fleming enlisted in Company 3 of the 10th Battalion Volunteer Militia Rifles in Toronto and was commissioned captain. The militia never did see action but Fleming mustered the men for drill every Friday night at the Northern Railway Freight House at the foot of Brock Street.

Fleming's job as engineer-in-chief drew to an end as work on the Northern Railway neared completion; he took leave of his engineering staff in January 1863, presenting them with a piece of the first sod he had pocketed in 1851, a portion of the bottle used in 1853 to christen the naming of Collingwood Harbour, and these words:

> It is one of the misfortunes of the profession to which I am proud to belong that our business is to make and not to enjoy; we no sooner make a rough place smooth than we move to another and fresh field, leaving others to enjoy what we have accomplished. We are, however, satisfied that it should be so; we take pleasure in having work to do, and a pride in it after it is done.

Fleming was a man of action, but he was also very much a sentimentalist, with a keen sense of history. Why else would he keep a piece of sod for twelve years, why else on his honeymoon would he gather up a lump of wood to fashion into a baby's cradle one day? The quality of looking forward yet keeping an attachment to the things of the past was a measure of Fleming's breadth of vision, and an attribute that endeared him to his associates.

Within a week Fleming was moving to a fresh field; the Canadian premier, Sandfield Macdonald, called him in to discuss the much-talked-about Intercolonial Railway scheme from Nova Scotia to Quebec, and even a railway to British Columbia, of which Fleming had become a well-known exponent. He first set out his ideas at a town hall meeting at Port Hope in 1858. Fleming had a vision of a great railway line one day spanning the northern half of North America entirely within British territory. If a national system made sense over the comparatively short distances of the United Kingdom, then all the more so here. He was under no illusions about the immensity of the proposal, surpassing in magnitude, cost, and physical difficulty any engineering project ever undertaken; far more daunting than the American experience. British America's population was small, the distances great and much of the terrain difficult. The colonial economy was captive to the vagaries of political and economic forces largely beyond its control – when fur hats were in vogue in Europe the price of skins soared, but when the fashion turned the bottom fell out of the fur trade; the timber trade boomed so long as

European ships were made of wood, but with the change to steel and iron, the logging camps and shipyards of New Brunswick and Quebec were hit hard. Immigrants flocked to the United States and it protected its growing markets and industries, making the fledgling Canadian factories subject to the fluctuations of foreign tariffs. Not even the British market could be taken for granted; some British politicians were calling for protected imperial trade but others advocated completely free trade with all nations. Canadian businessmen in the 1850s badly wanted to get a larger share of the lucrative United States market; the north-south trade was more interesting to them than trade with New Brunswick and Nova Scotia; as for transatlantic trade, the seaport of Portland, Maine, was closer to Montreal than was Halifax. Parochialism reigned in British America.

To Fleming, however, it was evident from the American example that where trains went the economy boomed: land values, wage levels, prices, and heavy machinery industries all were given a tremendous boost. He knew that villages and towns would spring up along the railway line as the newly opened central plains filled with settlers. Thousands of men would be needed to construct the railway, and their presence would further stimulate economic activity. Above all, a transcontinental railway would put an end to the regional isolation that plagued the colonies; social and commercial ties would grow with the railway, and in the process a greater sense of national identity would be born. Fleming elaborated on his views in a paper, "Practical Observations on the Construction of a Continuous Line of Railway from Canada to the Pacific Ocean on British Territory" published as an annex to Henry Youle Hind's Sketch of an Overland Route to British Columbia in 1862.

Fleming's advocacy of a transcontinental railway was noticed in the tiny settlers' outpost on the Red River in the western territories. The Red River colonists felt cut off and neglected by the mainstream of British American society; they desperately wanted an end to their isolation. The whole of the vast western region had been since 1670 the private preserve of the Hudson's Bay Company, which regarded it as a free range for the fur-bearing animals that were its mainstay. Settlers, with their fences and ploughs, were an unwelcome intrusion.

All this changed in 1810 when the Earl of Selkirk and a group of Scottish investors bought controlling interest in the Hudson's Bay Company; a year later Selkirk secured a grant of 18.2 million hectares in the Red River Valley to establish a farming settlement. The small farming community of largely Scottish settlers found themselves in bitter conflict with the Métis buffalo hunters and fur traders, whose way of life was threatened. Tension ran deep between those immigrants who wished to put down roots and farm the land and the mixed-race descendants of aboriginals and earlier European arrivals who wished to continue their free-ranging nomadic way of life following the buffalo. Time and the flow of immigration were on the settlers' side, and a confrontation between traditional and new ways of living on the plains was inevitable, particularly as too little effort was made to assuage the anxieties of the Métis. However, as awareness of the agricultural potential of the central plains grew, and with the discovery of gold in British Columbia's Fraser Valley in 1858, the days of Hudson's Bay Company control were numbered. By the 1860s the Red River Colony was impatient to share in the mainstream of British American life.

The proprietors of the colony's only newspaper, the *Nor'wester,* were familiar with Fleming's Port Hope address, and his persistent advocacy of a transcontinental railway; they proposed to the colonists that Fleming be approached to become their advocate in appealing for an end to isolation. A statement or "memorial" was approved at a public meeting and sent to Fleming in January 1863. The colonists wanted a means of transportation between the eastern provinces and British Columbia by way of Lake Superior, the Red River, and the Saskatchewan River. Although Fleming at this stage had never set eyes on the prairies, the colony's appeal was entirely consistent with his vision and he happily championed its cause.

The Red River Memorial outlined the practicability of a railway line across the easy terrain of the prairies, and the commercial advantage of thus extending the markets of Britain and Canada. The colonists pointed out the vast wealth of the Northwest in furs, gold, iron, lead, coal and petroleum; they elaborated on how the central plains, once opened to the east, would soon fill with settlers and become a counter to increasing American influence in the region. Therein were joined the main elements of the colony's appeal – freedom from the shackles of Hudson's Bay Company control, and defence against eventual absorption by the United States.

The lengthening shadow of the American giant in the midwest was seen by the Red River colonists as a political threat, and was also a source of discontent insofar as the growing prosperity of the American midwest emphasized the colony's stunted growth. They feared the intentions of an expansionist United States; it was anyone's guess what the United States would do once the Civil War was over. The central plains of the American midwest were rapidly filling up with settlers, and land-hungry Americans could not but be aware of the vast empty plains to the north. The British Columbia gold discoveries also tempted Americans to look north. The wounds of the 1812–14 war were healed, but scars remained; there were disconcerting noises coming from the United States about finishing the job begun in the American Revolution, and evicting the British from North America altogether. This threat touched a sensitive imperialist nerve in Fleming.

Sandford first submitted the Red River appeal to the Canadian premier, Sandfield Macdonald, and the governor general, Lord Monck, in March 1863. Two months later, he embarked on the steamship *United Kingdom* from Quebec City to carry the Red River case to London. This was Fleming's first extended separation from Jeanie and the children, and his first visit back to Britain since leaving nearly twenty years before. Sixteen days later – the voyage took six weeks less than his first crossing, in the *Brilliant* – Fleming was back in Scotland. In Kirkcaldy, with its store of memories, Shirra Ha still stood on Glasswork Street and his initials, carved on a tree trunk in the garden, still were clearly visible. The faces of the townsfolk, however, had altered: "I felt like Rip Van Winkle; a new generation had arisen. Not a single countenance did I recognize and certainly none knew me."

Fleming travelled by train from Scotland to London. It was his first visit to the great city, and he took in much sightseeing and theatre before his scheduled call on the colonial secretary, the Duke of Newcastle. Newcastle had visited Canada three years before with the Prince of Wales, and in fact had boarded Fleming's Northern Railway; the two men had hit it off well. Fleming urged on Newcastle the necessity of countering American influence, pointing out that the Americans already were providing the Red River colony with postal and steamboat services.

British America had to learn to walk before it could run. Fleming told Newcastle it would be best to begin with a territorial road and telegraph line to the Pacific coast. In time a railway would become practicable as settlements grew up along the road. Fleming's plan had the virtue of avoiding the costly duplication of surveys along separate routes for roads and railways. Newcastle listened with apparent interest, and Fleming went away hopeful. He returned home on the Great Eastern via New York; while there he found a copy of the Toronto *Globe* in his hotel and, as luck would have it, saw the birth announcement for his third daughter, Jeanie II.

In spite of the hopes raised by the mission to London, six years elapsed before the Hudson's Bay Company surrendered its control over the Northwest to the new Canadian government, thus permitting western development to begin in earnest. As late as 1868 the Red River settlement was still languishing in its isolation. It was hit by a plague of grasshoppers that year and Fleming wrote to his friend George Monro Grant, a clergyman of the Church of Scotland in Halifax, asking him to take up a collection for the victims. Their response was not generous: the Red River was even farther from the preoccupations of Nova Scotians than it was from Great Britain. As Grant said in his reply to Fleming: "I could have collected as much, and the people would have given as intelligently had the sufferers been in Abyssinia."

CHAPTER 3

INTERCOLONIAL BEGINNINGS

During the 1830s the international frontier between New Brunswick and Maine was the subject of a festering dispute, and anti-American sentiment ran high, aggravated by the incursions of organized bands of marauders crossing the border to wreak havoc. At the same time, the idea of intercolonial steam railway links between the Atlantic seaports of Nova Scotia and New Brunswick – notably Halifax, St. John, and St. Andrews – and Quebec and New England was actively promoted and some survey work done. Unfortunately, however, the preferred route ran across disputed territory. The boundary was not settled until 1842, but ironically the hostile atmosphere may have contributed to railway development. The British military authorities began thinking about building a military road as part of the system of British American defences; from this grew the notion that a railway, besides being of military value, could be of commercial benefit to the colonies. It was thought, however, that the principal beneficiaries should share in the associated costs, so the colonies were billed for a survey undertaken in 1848 by Major Robinson and other officers of the British Army.

Robinson favoured an eastern or coastal route along the New Brunswick shore, as far away as possible from the American border. From the colonies' point of view this was the worst option: the coast route was long and circuitous; it passed through little settled country and offered no reasonable prospect of a return on construction costs. Major Robinson's survey did not much matter however, because quibbling over routes and cost-sharing formulae among the colonies of Nova Scotia, New Brunswick, and Canada would continue, for many more years, to delay any prospect of a railway. The financially strapped imperial government, weighed down by the Crimean War, was too hard pressed to help, and the financial difficulties of Canada's Grand Trunk Railway, intended to tap the American trade and connect Montreal and Toronto, offered scant encouragement to its London investors to back a railway line through the sparsely populated maritime provinces. As for the Province of Canada, there was no obvious commercial advantage in a railway line through the uninhabited hinterland of New Brunswick to the seaport of Halifax when Portland, Maine, offered the same advantage at half the distance from Montreal. With an intercolonial railway plan thus bogged down in seemingly endless haggling, the separate colonies proceeded to build their own railway lines in the 1850s.

American history intervened in 1861, however, to do more than politicians had managed in a decade to advance the cause of an intercolonial railway. In November, with the Civil War raging, an American warship intercepted the British mail packet *Trent* on the high seas, boarded her at gunpoint and removed two Confederate agents. A wave of indignation swept the United Kingdom, and garrisons in British America were hastily reinforced with the despatch of 14,000 troops; most of the soldiers arrived in the dead of winter and with the St. Lawrence frozen over, suffered a long, cold march through the desolate forests of New Brunswick. The strategic advantage of a railway line from Halifax now was unmistakably obvious, and an intercolonial railway took on pressing military importance, even if it still lacked commercial sense. Still, however, Canadian foot-dragging over cost-sharing stood in the way of progress.

The Maritime provinces by now were thoroughly fed up with the Canadians' continued prevarication; the New Brunswick premier, Leonard Tilley, showed his disgust in a letter to the colony's lieutenant-governor:

> The real trouble in Canada is that in the Eastern Section, a portion of the population, of French origin, think the Railway will lead to the Union of the Provinces, and the destruction of their power and political influence ... in Eastern Canada there is a strong feeling against the Railway, first because they now have two outlets in winter, New York and Portland, and a third in summer by the St. Lawrence; secondly, because no portion of the road is to be built or money expended in Canada West, and the last, but by no means the least, is the prejudice against the management of the construction of the Grand Trunk Railway.[1]

The colonies were able to agree that an exploratory survey and initial cost estimate for an intercolonial railway should be undertaken. Fleming was chosen by Canada's premier, Sandfield Macdonald, to represent his province on a three-person commission of engineers: Nova Scotia and New Brunswick were asked to appoint an engineer, as was the imperial government. In the event all the parties agreed that Fleming could represent them all. But once again they fell out over which one should pay how much. In the end the Province of Canada decided to go it alone and foot the bill itself. Sandfield Macdonald turned the job over to Fleming, offering him the then substantial salary of $4,800 per annum – only $200 less than a minister's wage.

There was a great deal of public interest in the adventurous expedition. When Fleming was organizing the survey, a man approached him for a job and was taken on as a trail-blazer at one dollar a day. He gave his address as Government House, Fredericton. Soon after, Fleming received a letter from his new employee reporting that he could not now join the survey, as he had become the Earl of Aberdeen owing to the death of the previous earl.

Fleming and his survey crew set out from Quebec City on 5 March 1864 (typically, he was ahead of the bureaucrats: his letter of appointment did not arrive until a week after he left); travelling on snowshoes and by dogsled through the New Brunswick forests, they advanced with amazing speed from Rivière-du-Loup down the Matapedia Valley via Restigouche, Dalhousie, Bathurst, and Chatham to the provincial capital, Fredericton. They travelled light, living off the land with its abundance of partridge, porcupine, and moose.

Canada's Grand Trunk Railway and its general manager, Charles J. Brydges, had been interested in the projected intercolonial railway for some time. The GTR terminated at Rivière-du-Loup, and had no all-year access to the sea except through American territory to Portland, Maine. It was essential to Brydges that a route through British territory be secured for his railway, in face of the threatening hostility of the northern states after the Civil War. Brydges also was unsettled by a proposal for a Portland-to-Halifax railway line advanced by American interests; if the Maritime provinces went this route Brydges' GTR risked being barred from the ice-free maritime ports. Brydges accordingly wrote to Tilley, and to Nova Scotia's premier, Charles Tupper, proposing to form a company with parties in Britain to build the line from Rivière-du-Loup to Truro, Nova Scotia, on the basis of Fleming's surveys. Brydges' proposed company was to be aided by provincial subsidies backed by the imperial government. The premiers turned down his offer; Fleming's surveys were nowhere near complete, and so negotiations would be premature. Brydges was absolutely opposed to the provinces proceeding with their own piecemeal construction projects, fearing that the most lucrative sections of the intercolonial line would be hived off, with his GTR left to operate the remainder.

Tupper, though, was under enormous political pressure to get on with awarding construction contracts for sections within Nova Scotia, including a Truro-to-Moncton link through his own county, a line from Windsor to Annapolis, and another from Truro to Pictou. The demand for the Pictou Railway was particularly urgent; Tupper's chief commissioner of railways, James McDonald, was from Pictou and he wielded great influence in government circles.

In fact, a Truro-to-Pictou extension had its own attractions; in particular, the possibility of enhanced trade with Prince Edward Island from Pictou Harbour, bearing in mind that New Brunswick had already extended a line to the Northumberland Strait. Tupper needed a chief engineer who would drive his railway projects forward. The first and most obvious person to come to mind was Sandford Fleming, whom Tupper had often met on intercolonial survey matters. He enticed Fleming with the promise of several years' railway construction work in Nova Scotia, whereas, judging from the poor-mouthing of the Intercolonial project in the Canadian legislature, its prospects were in doubt – or at least that is what Tupper suggested to Fleming. Fleming accepted Tupper's offer on a part-time basis while continuing with what was now officially known as the Intercolonial Railway Company.

With Tupper pressing him so hard to get on with the Nova Scotia projects, Fleming realized that he had to be based closer to the field operations there. Accordingly, he collected Jeanie and the children in Toronto, sold off the furniture, and moved them to Halifax; it was to be their home for the next five years. Two more children were born to them in Halifax – their daughter Maude in 1867, who died a year later (another daughter, Jeanie II, was also to die in infancy), and their son Walter, in 1868. Tupper and Fleming became fast friends; the premier was also a medical doctor and became family physician to the Fleming family. The two men schemed to develop resources in Tupper's part of the province, and became business partners in Springhill coal and Cumberland salt ventures. Sandford and Jeanie thus found themselves at the pinnacle of Halifax society. They were always invited to parties at Government House.

Fleming's dearest friend, however, was the clergyman at St. Matthew's Presbyterian Church, George Monro Grant, a Scotsman like himself. Grant was born in Nova Scotia in 1835, the son of a Banffshire settler. Fleming and Grant could not have been more different in outward appearance, except for their full beards – Fleming tall, and burly now, well over ninety kilograms, Grant slight and wiry, missing his right hand as a result of a boyhood prank in a coal mine. Grant had enormous energy, and was as quick and voluble in conversation as Fleming was gentle and measured. In outlook the two shared a great deal; both were devout Presbyterians and fervent advocates of Canadian and imperial unity, even when these political views were unpopular in Nova Scotia. They remained close friends for the rest of their lives.

Less than a year after Fleming began work on the Intercolonial, he submitted his survey report. By February 1865 he had examined no less than fifteen routes in an incredibly short period of time – three along the international frontier with Maine, nine through central New Brunswick, and three along the north shore of the province. Quite clearly there would be objections, on military grounds, to a line near the American border. As for the central and northern routes, all manner of parochial interests clamoured for the one that ran closest to their particular town, mine, or sawmill. Fleming concluded on commercial grounds that a north shore line along the Baie des Chaleurs was to be preferred, since it was 100 kilometres nearer to Liverpool, England, than was Halifax, and 424 kilometres nearer to Montreal. His advocacy of a major seaport at Shippegan on the Baie des Chaleurs was not calculated to win friends in Halifax, but as Fleming conceived it, the eventual extension of the Intercolonial Railway line across Newfoundland to St. John's would facilitate the shortest possible ocean crossing; steamships would dock at St. John's, and their cargo would speed by rail across the island to the Gulf coast for transfer to steamers to Shippegan. A further key element of Fleming's plan was a spur line south from the Intercolonial, to connect with the American railway system.

Fleming's commitment to Tupper to get the Pictou extension open was also very much on his mind all during this time. Most of the construction contracts were let by the end of 1864 but the work was falling badly behind schedule. Fleming told Tupper that without drastic action the line would not open until 1868, but with confederation plans afoot, Tupper could not wait that long. He wanted to be absolutely certain the Pictou line would be subsumed in the Intercolonial project. Tupper also had his eye on the political calendar: a provincial election was due in 1867. He asked Fleming if there was any way the line could be open by 1 May 1867. Fleming told Tupper that he could deliver on time, provided the construction was turned over to him exclusively. His proposed plan of action was both startling and innovative – he would bring in steam excavators to speed the heavy earth cuttings, roof over and enclose sites so work could continue in winter, and string a telegraph line the length of the work to speed communications: all daring, all costly.

Tupper and Fleming concluded a secret pact in December 1865, whereby Fleming offered to become the sole contractor for the Pictou Railway, and to build it for $100,000 less than the estimates of the year previous. Tupper wrote to a civil engineer, Alexander Macnab, to ask if in his view it would be in the public interest to accept Fleming's offer; Macnab responded, almost by return, that Fleming's cost estimate was unbeatable. Only then, with the deal sewn up and with no apparent regard for what might easily have been seen as a conflict of interest, Fleming resigned his government post as the province's chief engineer and assumed the construction contract. And who should succeed him but the same Mr. Macnab, who had commented so quickly and so favourably on the contract proposal. The sole-contract arrangement with Fleming was at the expense of the contractors who until then had been engaged on the Pictou Railway, several of whom had political influence in

Colchester and Pictou counties. Indeed, the leader of the opposition in the provincial legislature, A.G. Archibald, was the representative for Colchester county. With his own contract still a secret, Fleming – acting apparently in his capacity as chief engineer – negotiated an end to the existing contracts.

Tupper's announcement of the new arrangement with Fleming in February 1866 ignited a firestorm of indignation in the Nova Scotia assembly. The opposition Liberals under Archibald were incensed at the highly irregular and quite possibly illegal dealings that had come to light. Archibald stood up in the assembly chamber on 15 March to move a vote of censure in the government; he heaped scorn on Tupper.

> The Government of this country, the men to whom you have entrusted the interests of Nova Scotia, descending to the miserable position of the pettiest criminal offender, have, for two months carried on the affairs of a great public department under false pretenses – have been holding out a man as their engineer who was no engineer, and using him in the name of a disinterested agent, but with the reality of an interested contractor, to impose upon and deceive the entire community.[2]

Archibald alleged that Tupper had ignored the provincial law requiring that all public works be advertised; what about the impropriety or indeed illegality of summarily cancelling existing arrangements with contractors, he asked; why was Fleming not required to put up any security as a guarantee against his contract, as stipulated in provincial law; was Alexander Macnab promised the chief engineer's job for having recommended Fleming's offer to the government?

The opposition derided the terms of Fleming's contract, which, they argued, could only come within the original estimate because Fleming had shaved off some of the earlier specifications. He had reduced the width of the road bed, changed gradients and curves, reduced the weight of rails and quantity of ballast; had shaved off in excess of $200,000 by cutting corners. In any event, Archibald claimed, Fleming's original estimates were high compared with similar estimates for the Intercolonial.

Tupper would have none of this; he argued boldly that Nova Scotia was getting a bargain by having Fleming deliver the railway on time and within the original cost estimates, something the original contractors could not do. He told a sceptical assembly that Fleming had been prepared to put up financial guarantees, but rigid adherence to this contract principle would have pushed up the price, since they inevitably would have been written into the

Sandford Fleming in mid-life.
National Archives of Canada, PA 26427

Sandford Fleming in 1845, the year he emigrated to Canada. A tide of British immigrants poured into British North America in the 1840s; the population of what is now Ontario doubled within the decade to 950,000.

National Archives of Canada, C 8692

Home of Dr. Hutchison in Peterborough, Ontario. A Scotsman who made good in the New World, he visited his old home in Fifeshire with accounts of the wonderful prospects in Canada. The Flemings, father and sons, were inspired to try their luck. It was here in the Hutchison house that Fleming first unpacked his sea trunk to begin a new life.

National Archives of Canada, C 33155

When Fleming, newly arrived from Scotland, first set eyes on Queen's College at Kingston in 1845, he could scarcely have imagined that thirty-five years later he would become its chancellor – a remarkable tribute to a man who himself had no university education. It could not have hurt, of course, that his dearest friend, George Grant, had been appointed principal three years earlier.

National Archives of Canada, PA 122648

Fleming was witness to the torching of the Parliament Building in Montreal in 1849. A mob of 1,500 ransacked the building, hurled the mace out of a window, and set the structure alight. Firemen were prevented from getting near, and the hose was cut. The Parliament Building was soon engulfed in flames. Not able to reach the parliamentary library to save some of the books, Fleming burst into the Legislative Council chamber and, with three others, rescued the large portrait of Queen Victoria from its place over the Speaker's chair. The painting's heavy frame had to be discarded, but as for the crown that surmounted it, Fleming recorded, "I had the honour of sleeping last night with the crown in my bedroom."

McCord Museum of Canadian History, Montreal

Charles J. Brydges of the Grand Trunk Railway. Brydges, confidant of Prime Minister John A. Macdonald, wanted badly to see the Intercolonial Railway started in the interest of extra business for his railway, which was in financial difficulties. He wrote to Macdonald on New Year's Day, 1867: "I hope you are not losing sight of Intercolonial, although of course I know you won't. I hear a good deal about the work being done by commissioners whose appointment shall be confirmed by the imperial government. If so the men will need to be very carefully selected." Who should subsequently become one of the board of commissioners to oversee Intercolonial construction but the same C.J. Brydges. He locked horns with the Intercolonial's chief engineer, Fleming, over many issues and, annoyed by Fleming's persistent appeals to the prime minister over the heads of the commissioners, wrote to Macdonald to rake up old rumours about collusion and profiteering on the Pictou portion of the Nova Scotia Railway: "Howe told me that he and his party were exceedingly afraid of Fleming, and that they had the greatest difficulty in bringing themselves to consent to his position, arising out of what they felt were grave errors – to use mild terms – in the Pictou matter."
National Archives of Canada, C 948

Survey crews on the Intercolonial Railway lived a rugged and sparse existence. Provisions were meagre – a bit of bacon, a box of dried herring perhaps, some hard biscuit, a sack of tea, and sugar. Indians were hired as guides through the nearly impenetrable forests. Crews slept under canvas, often in the most miserable conditions, suffering from the extreme cold in winter and plagued by relentless onslaughts of black flies in summer. Fleming's travel journal describes a typical campsite on the Matapedia River: "At six o'clock we camped at a pretty rocky place by the edge of a rapid. The Indians hauled up the canoe and at once proceeded to erect the tent and prepare for supper while I refreshed myself with a delightful bath in a clear, rocky basin quite near our camp, deep enough to swim and as smooth as crystal. The black and sand flies soon became very troublesome so I tried for the first time what I brought as mosquito oil, besmearing my hands, face and neck with it, and certainly had some relief. We soon had supper – fried bacon, hard biscuit and good strong black tea, finishing as usual with a smoke. The Indians washed our two dishes, one single spoon, knife and fork, brought spruce boughs from the woods to make our bed on the gravel beach, collected dry wood to make a good fire in front of the tent during the night whilst I wandered amongst the rocks. We then all rested awhile before going to sleep. I then lay down under canvas, my feet to the fire and an Indian on each side of me."

National Archives of Canada, C 17695

Were the bridges on the Intercolonial Railway to be built of iron or wood? This question became a battle royal between Fleming and the overseeing board of commissioners. Fleming believed that wood, with its ever-present risk of fire from sparks belching from train engines, was a false economy. He wrote to the prime minister: "I can only see one argument in favor of the adoption of wooden bridges, and that argument can only be used by those who view the union of the provinces as an experiment very likely to prove unsuccessful. If there is any possibility of the railway being allowed in a few years to fall into disuse, then make, not only the bridges, but everything else as primitive and temporary as possible; or, perhaps better still, build no railway at all. If on the other hand, the government have any faith in the union, and believe as I do that it is destined to last, then it will be studying true economy to make the railway as durable, substantial, reliable and permanent as possible."

National Archives of Canada, C 18189

Charles Tupper, medical doctor, provincial premier, federal minister, diplomat and prime minister. His friendship with Fleming became an unbearable political liability for the government and for himself – he was obliged ultimately to forsake his old friend. It was rumoured that in the early days of railway construction in Nova Scotia, he and Fleming literally were as thick as thieves in turning the Pictou Railway portion to their personal profit.
National Archives of Canada, PA 26673

Alexander Mackenzie. Railway scandal felled Canada's first prime minister, and Mackenzie was summoned to form a government in 1873. Mackenzie was born in Perthshire, Scotland, and came to Canada in 1842 as a journeyman stonecutter. His days as prime minister were dogged by economic recession and a fractious political party, important parts of which believed that the transcontinental railway commitment imposed an intolerable burden on the fledgling country. His unhappy tenure as prime minister was cut short after one term in office by a resurgent John A. Macdonald.
National Archives of Canada, PA 26522

Lord Dufferin, the Queen's representative in Canada, and the British colonial secretary, Lord Carnarvon, became enmeshed in Canadian railway controversy, provoking a historic confrontation with the prime minister, Alexander Mackenzie, who was not about to brook continued interference in domestic matters by imperial authorities. The flamboyant Ulster nobleman Dufferin, for his part, was never enamoured of the stolid Scot Mackenzie. He wrote to Carnarvon shortly after the 1874 election: "Mr. Mackenzie, my prime minister, was originally a stone mason – he is by no means a man of genius, but he is industrious, conscientious and exact."

National Archives of Canada, C 24078

Marcus Smith, Fleming's associate since
Intercolonial Railway days and his deputy in
British Columbia, turned to implacable foe
when he failed to have his way on his pre-
ferred more northerly route through the
Rockies and across British Columbia. He
waged an unceasing campaign of invective
and innuendo to discredit Fleming and the
Mackenzie government.
National Archives of Canada, PA 25443

Indian camp near Carlton, Saskatchewan, 1871. George Grant, secretary on Fleming's great overland trek to the Pacific coast in 1872, was sensitive to the dislocation that railway construction and settlement would bring to the native peoples' ways of living: "And now a foreign race is swarming over the country, to mark out lines, to erect fences, and to say 'This is mine and not yours,' till not an inch shall be left the original owner. All this may be inevitable. But in the name of justice, of doing as we would be done by, of the 'sacred rights' of property, is not the Indian entitled to liberal, and, if possible, permanent compensation?"
National Archives of Canada, C 80069

Left to right: James Robertson Ross, adjutant general of the militia; Halifax physician Dr. Arthur Moren; Sandford Fleming; clergyman George Grant (concealing his missing hand); and Sandford's eldest son, Franky. They had gathered at the Queen's Hotel, Toronto, in mid-July 1872 before setting out on their trek westward to the Pacific coast, the account of which is recorded in Grant's picturesque travelogue *Ocean to Ocean.*
National Archives of Canada, C 66559

Locomotive and carriages at opening of Pembina branch line linking Winnipeg with the CPR in 1878. The train had arrived in the Prairies. The Pembina branch was constructed along the Red River from Emerson on the U.S. border. Ownership of the line was transferred to the new CPR company as part of the contract terms.
National Archives of Canada, C 1173

Rock cut near Winstons, Ontario. Construction crews had to blast their way through solid rock on many sections, at great risk to life and limb.
National Archives of Canada, C 21982

Railway construction workers' bunkhouse. Determined to get the railway line through to the Pacific coast years ahead of schedule in one of the world's great engineering feats, General Manager William Cornelius Van Horne pumped thousands upon thousands of labourers into the works. He drove them to track-laying records that, combined with short cuts, made it possible to achieve his goal an incredible five years short of the deadline.
National Archives of Canada, PA 115432

Fleming was embarrassed by his lack of academic qualifications when he was elected chancellor of Queen's College. The university principal and his good friend, George Grant, gave him some advice on an inaugural address: "A few wise words are better than volumes of platitudes, and you can give those – something on the true object of all true education, namely, learning how to learn and how to work, in order that our natures may be fitly developed and that our lives may be fruitful, or something on the special needs of our country and our time; or some lessons of experience and meditation thereupon."
National Archives of Canada, C 14068

The CPR waged a vigorous campaign to entice prospective migrants from Britain to the newly opening West. This advertisement features the agricultural potential of Manitoba. The population of Manitoba grew from 25,228 in 1871 to 62,260 in 1881 and 152,506 in 1891.

Glenbow Archives, Calgary, Alberta, NA 2222-1

Sailor Bar Bluff (twelve kilometres above Yale, B.C., where construction began in 1880), looking down the valley.

Canadian Pacific Archives, 25761

Engineering party at the summit, Rocky Mountains, November 1883.
Canadian Pacific Archives, 1359

Engineering party at Moberly House, Columbia Valley, B.C., November 1884.
Canadian Pacific Archives, 1341

final cost. As for the secrecy attached to the awarding of the contract, Tupper explained that it was done in this fashion to ensure that the government concluded the best possible settlements with the former contractors.

The opposition were not in the slightest convinced; they impugned Fleming's honesty, pointing out that Fleming allowed an estimated $140,000 for iron girders, when in fact there were only two main bridges on the entire Pictou line, costing $14,500. The government easily turned aside the censure motion, but the opposition had done its damage. Tupper and Fleming were left with a legacy of mistrust that would shadow them for years to come. However, Tupper did get his Pictou Railway on time and within estimate, and Fleming had grown suddenly very wealthy – whether from the proceeds of his private business deals with Tupper or otherwise is a matter of conjecture. His private papers for the period record large transfers of spare cash – $15,000 to his father-in-law to invest for him, $40,000 to his bank account in Montreal, £16,000 to a Kirkcaldy bank account, and the purchase of $40,000 of Northern Railway bonds. Fleming bought property in Montreal and paid £17,000 for a new collier ship which he ran between Pictou Harbour and Montreal with coal shipments. He urged his brother, David, to open a coal yard in Montreal to stock coal that was not sold immediately from dock side. Fleming paid $4,000 to Tupper for the balance due on a coal mining venture in Cumberland County; he bought David's farm in Weston in 1869 and gave it to his sister, Jane; and the following year he bought several lots of prime land on the Northwest Arm of Halifax, amassing nearly 41 hectares. It bears recalling that Fleming's annual salary on the Intercolonial was $4,800.

Fleming did work feverishly to get the Pictou line open; moving constantly between Halifax and the railway works, sometimes with his eldest son, Franky. He coaxed and cajoled his men to greater efforts and showed no hesitation in resorting to unorthodox business practices.

> Finding the time passed for the completion of the grading in this section and a great deal remaining to be done, I proposed to Mitchell Company on August 4, 1866 that instead of deducting the penalty under the Contract I would, provided they proceeded vigorously with their work and finished the whole section by the 15th October following, pay them a handsome bonus.

The works were plagued by persistent heavy rains for the greater part of the 1866 season but, nevertheless, by the end of the year only 10 percent of the work remained to be done. In spite of opposition charges of second-rate building materials and specifications, the ever-obliging provincial railway engineer, Mr. Macnab, reported to the government in March 1867: "The character of the masonry which has been constructed on the Pictou railway, both as regards the quality of material and style of workmanship, is of the most superior description, and warrants the assertion that a better class of work does not exist on any railway in America."[3]

The Pictou Railway was officially opened on 31 May 1867, although there was still work to be done before it could be considered complete. The complaints against Fleming, including charges of poor construction and excessive profits, lingered; years later Canada's minister of justice, John Thompson, wrote to the prime minister, Macdonald:

> In twenty-three years observation of Fleming – beginning with his robbery of Nova Scotia to the extent of his whole fortune by breach of trust ... I have never been able to regard him otherwise than as the great example which Canada presents of successful dishonesty and conceit.[4]

In these formative days of a Canadian national identity, there was a certain synergism between politics, business, and the press. In a fast-changing society there was everything to play for as alliances formed, dissolved, and re-formed; political patronage, insider dealing, and conflict of interest were common, the unwritten rules of the game. Still, public morality would not allow them to be acknowledged or condoned as such, and that is why they provided such handy ammunition for opposition by politicians and the press.

With the Pictou Railway project out of the way, Fleming took Jeanie, the children and Jeanie's parents on a holiday to Europe, but their happiness was marred by the death of Jeanie's mother on the outbound voyage, and the death of their baby daughter Maude on the way home. In Europe, Fleming took his family to see his native Kirkcaldy, and they crossed over to Paris where they went up in a hot air balloon. Fleming's railway engineering career was flying every bit as high.

CHAPTER 4

THE FIRST NATIONAL
UNDERTAKING

Fleming's exploratory surveys were an essential preliminary, but construction of the Intercolonial Railway would only begin when the colonies saw that it was more in their interest to cooperate than to go it alone. As the 1860s unfolded it became apparent that if the British American colonies did not hang together, they might well hang separately.

With the American Civil War drawing to a close, there was great anxiety in British North America about the designs of an aggressive post-war United States; some Americans were making angry noises about exacting their pound of flesh for what they saw as active British sympathy for the Confederate cause. Some said Canada was full of Confederate sympathizers; perhaps this was the moment to evict the British from North America once and for all. Then there were the Fenians, a group of Irishmen dedicated to the liberation of their homeland who were making threatening noises about a military campaign against the English in the Province of Canada and other British colonies. On top of everything else, in 1865 the United States abrogated the reciprocal trade treaty that had stood between itself and the British colonies since 1854. It would be no easy task to hold the line at the international frontier against a determined assault. Steps had to be taken to buttress British America's independent future.

Fleming and the Montreal politician Thomas D'Arcy McGee became acquainted in Quebec in 1864. McGee was a leading exponent of British American union. He and Fleming both were exasperated by the constant bickering and parochialism of the provinces standing in the way of union. Fleming thought the greatest obstacle was in the fact that the people of the separate provinces really did not know each other well; there was all too little communication and no significant commerce between them. He asked McGee whether a visit to the Maritime provinces by Canada's politicians and press might not help break down some of the barriers; Fleming would be going to the Maritimes in a few days and offered to try to fix things at that end. McGee undertook to do what he could with the Canadians. Fleming carried his proposal to the sympathetic ear of Tupper in Halifax, and managed to solicit the necessary invitations to the Canadians from the Halifax and St. John boards of trade. McGee was less successful in getting the Canadian legislature to accept as a body, but several of the leaders would soon be going east, in any event, for the Charlottetown conference; they with several others, some forty assembly members, twenty-five from the legislative council, and forty others, mostly from the Canadian papers, went in their individual capacity. The visit set the stage for the Charlottetown conference.

Delegates from Nova Scotia, New Brunswick, and Prince Edward Island had decided to meet in Charlottetown in September to discuss the possibility of a closer association among themselves. In June, the governor general asked if Canadian delegates might join them to discuss a more ambitious union. A month after the expanded Charlottetown conference, the meeting reconvened at Quebec City and there were passed seventy-two resolutions on federation including the following:

> The General Government shall secure without delay, the completion of the Intercolonial Railway from Rivière-du-Loup through New Brunswick to Truro in Nova Scotia.

The railway plan became a condition of confederation, but the agreement on it was fragile. John A. Macdonald of Canada wrote to Tupper on 14 November:

> It is of the utmost importance that between now and the time of the meeting of Parliament nothing should be done to strengthen the hands of the Opposition, or to give them the opportunity of getting up a new cry. With this view, I cannot too strongly impress on you the necessity of carrying out the policy of not in any way giving any party the slightest control over the construction of any portion of the Intercolonial Railway ... Were it suspected that any considerable portion of the road for which Canada is going to pledge itself was given away to contractors without the consent or sanction of the Government, a storm would at once arise which could not be allayed, and would peril the whole scheme.[1]

Tupper, of course, was anxious to get work started within his own province, on as much of the line as possible, knowing full well its importance in bringing a reluctant Nova Scotia into the proposed union. He told

Macdonald that it would be politically damaging to himself if he were not able to strike a bargain with Brydges, as soon as possible, for construction of the Truro-to-Moncton line.

The Quebec Resolutions were submitted to the imperial government and the imperial Parliament passed the British North America Act in February 1867, making possible Canada's Confederation on 1 July. The act acknowledged that construction of the Intercolonial Railway was an essential precondition for the entry of Nova Scotia and New Brunswick into the union and that therefore its commencement should be within six months.

There were advantages to the imperial government in proceeding with the railway within Confederation. It would no longer be necessary to haggle with the separate provinces; the entire construction loan could be contracted by the new federal government. Nor would it be necessary to worry that any one province might back out of the project at any time. The imperial Parliament passed a Canada Railway Loan Act in April 1867, authorizing the guarantee of a Canadian loan up to £3 million for the Intercolonial's construction. The new Dominion Parliament in turn was required to pass an intercolonial railway act for a line to be approved by the imperial government, and with provision for its use by British troops. The Canadian government then placed a loan for £2 million on the London market.

Not everyone, however, was convinced of the need or desirability of the Intercolonial, particularly in Ontario, which was expected to pay the largest share of the costs, and yet seemed to stand to gain least from it. The most persistent Ontario sceptic was the federal member for Leeds North and Grenville North, Francis Jones, whose contrary views were only reinforced by the widespread post-Confederation dissatisfaction with the new union in Nova Scotia. Speaking in the House of Commons in March 1868, Jones said that if the Union was not to last, it would be wrong to proceed with the railway. The prime minister, John A. Macdonald, counselled Jones that unions always got off to a shaky start – witness the Scottish union with England – and warned that the process was not helped by talk of backing out of an agreement that was one of the cornerstones of the Canadian union.

No one was more anxious to see the Intercolonial Railway project started than Brydges of the GTR. His own railway was in financial difficulty, and he badly needed the extra business from a connection with the Intercolonial. Portland, Maine, was the GTR's winter outlet to the sea but it was no rival to New York for the European trade. Brydges had contacts on his side; he was very close to Macdonald. In 1867 there had been an effort to persuade Brydges to stand as a candidate in the elections, but he resisted, concerned perhaps that the fortunes of the GTR could be compromised if he had to accept the constraints of public office.

The federal government was no less anxious to press on with the Intercolonial, to dispel the alarming tide of anti-union sentiment in the Maritime provinces. The choice of routes had narrowed to three possibilities: the northern or Baie des Chaleurs route, a frontier route along the St. John River Valley close to the United States border, or a third running in a more central direction through New Brunswick. Since the imperial government's financial backing depended on London's approval of the route, the insecure frontier line was never really in the running. Powerful political forces lined up behind the others – Macdonald's minister of customs, Tilley, and his minister of public works, William MacDougall, favoured the central route, which was the most direct and would be least expensive to build; it was also the best from the commercial point of view. On the other hand, the minister of marine and fisheries, Peter Mitchell, from Northumberland, New Brunswick, favoured the northern route in the interest of the lower counties of Quebec and the north shore counties of New Brunswick. Fleming too was a strong backer of the northern route, and came down squarely in its favour in his survey report to the government. Macdonald had to steer through this minefield of competing interests, but in July 1868 cabinet adopted the northern route. The disgruntled public works minister, MacDougall, alleged in 1870 that Cartier and Mitchell had forced Macdonald to agree to the longer, northern route, with its 208 extra kilometres, as their price for consent to the acquisition of the western territories from the Hudson's Bay Company.

Within a week of Dominion Day, 1 July 1867, the federal government instructed Fleming to proceed with surveys to fix the exact location of the line. Fleming was relieved that the Pictou Railway controversy had not unduly blotted his copybook with the Ottawa authorities. He wrote to the public works minister on 25 October.

> I frankly confess that I had some fears lest a feeling might have arisen against me on account of the Pictou Railway affair. I knew that unfriendly persons would very naturally endeavour to make capital out of it against me and being at a distance I am in no position to defend myself. I am not ashamed of my connection with the Pictou Railway; indeed I have good reason to be proud of it. I have been the humble means of serving the Govt and Province of Nova Scotia *well* in connection therewith and this I am sure even those will admit who at one time were the stringent opponents of the Pictou Railway policy. I am not a Contractor by profession and do not wish to be considered one although in this instance circumstances made me nominally one, but by con-

senting to become one I am sure the Province was saved not less a sum that half a million dollars besides endless complications and difficulties.[2]

Fleming's resumed survey gave licence to every local interest between Truro and Rivière-du-Loup to stake a claim, since the line's location could make or break a community or business. The political pressures were enormous, and more than once Fleming was obliged to bow to them, one notable example being a circuitous sweep past the village of Dorchester, New Brunswick, which just happened to be the home of New Brunswick's representative on the Intercolonial Board of Commissioners and former provincial premier, E.B. Chandler.

Detailed surveys continued through 1867–68; Fleming set up an efficient and well-managed staff with delegated responsibilities organized in four separate districts – the St. Lawrence (207.2 km), Restigouche (204), Miramichi (183.2), and Nova Scotia (187.2), each assigned to a divisional engineer. The districts in turn were divided into several sections, each allocated to a resident engineer, two assistants, two rodmen and two chainmen. The survey parties hired axemen to blaze trails and labourers as required. The men generally lived in tents, summer and winter, and were kept supplied with food and other provisions by a commissariat officer for each district, who was also paymaster and accountant.

A four-man board of commissioners was set up in December 1868 to assume overall management and control of the Intercolonial project; the board had authority for all hirings and firings, except for Fleming's position which was a direct appointment by government. The commissioners' jobs, which promised to be rich in patronage power, went to trusted friends of the government – Tupper was offered the chair in recognition of his vigorous advocacy of union, but he turned it down for fear it would weaken his influence in combating the strong anti-Confederation movement in Nova Scotia. The chair thus went to the member of Parliament for North Norfolk, Ontario, Aquila Walsh. A former premier of New Brunswick and early champion of an intercolonial railway, Edward Chandler, was appointed, and so was Macdonald's GTR friend, C.J. Brydges. W.F. Coffin of Montreal was appointed but soon resigned, and was replaced by the federal member for Colchester County, Nova Scotia, A.W. McLelan.

The commissioners held their first meeting on 17 December, and two days later notified Fleming by telegram that he was to prepare new construction specifications and contract terms. Fleming was perplexed; he had already submitted detailed specifications, and contracts were about to be let to begin construction. He and his four district engineers lost no time in travelling to St. John for a first meeting with the commissioners on 29 December; it was apparent that there would be serious problems, from the outset, as the board sought to impose its will. Differences arose over the board's hiring practices, the basis on which contracts were let, and the construction of bridges. The patronage practices were particularly galling to Fleming. He had no control over the hiring and firing of his own staff, but was expected to make do even if appointees were unsuited for the job. The board informed him in April 1869 that certain of his engineers would be replaced, and that in future the commissioners would appoint the surveyors.

Fleming and the board were soon sharply divided over the manner of letting construction contracts. On Fleming's recommendation the government had already agreed to construct the railway in 32-kilometre sections, with work contracted by measurement and price in a schedule contract whereby the builder would be paid according to the exact work performed – land fill at one price, rock fill at another, etc. The schedule system was predicated on the fact that every kilometre of construction would have its own peculiarities, making it impossible to accurately estimate in advance the work required. The commissioners had other ideas, and swept aside the schedule system in favour of a bulk or distance system, whereby contractors were paid a fixed price, with tenders based on specifications determined by the chief engineer. The distance system placed a heavy burden on Fleming's engineering staff to make accurate profiles of the work to be done, to allow contractors to submit well-founded tenders. This in turn would slow down the surveyors' work and delay construction, even though the government wanted to get portions of the line under contract as soon as possible. The distance system was risky for the contractor: it made no provision for unexpected difficulties, so the contractor lost if the work turned out to be more than had been foreseen, and profited if things went unexpectedly easily. The board, though, thought otherwise, considering that the fixed cost system would avoid cost overruns by requiring contractors to stick to their tendered prices. It ignored Fleming's warning that contractors would inevitably pad their estimates to cover themselves for the unexpected.

Charles Brydges, commissioner and friend of the prime minister, wrote to Macdonald in January 1869, in a letter clearly intended to impugn Fleming's motives:

> I am entirely unable on either scientific or economical
> grounds, to understand Fleming's objection to contracts at
> so much per mile. All experience has proved that contracts
> at a schedule of prices, mean a vastly increased expenditure,
> an endless payment for extras and political difficulty.

The experience of the Pictou Line, must satisfy any impartial observer, so strong is the effect of that experience in the Lower Provinces ... Howe (of Nova Scotia) told me that he and his party were exceedingly afraid of Fleming, and that they had the greatest difficulty in bringing themselves to consent to his position, arising out of what they felt were grave errors-to use mild terms-in the Pictou matter.

I was somewhat surprised to hear that Mr. Schreiber [Fleming's head man on the Intercolonial] had resigned his position for the purpose of tendering for the construction of some portions, at any rate of the work. On the schedule of quantity principle he would have an enormous advantage over any other party making a tender, and to my mind this opens questions which I may think about but would rather not express definite opinion upon at present.[3]

Brydges was ruthless in probing Fleming's soft spot.

The most celebrated feud between Fleming and the commissioners was over the construction of bridges; Fleming had recommended that all intercolonial bridges be of iron, but the board proposed that they be constructed of much less expensive pine. Fleming told Macdonald the board was shortsighted; the once abundant pine forests of the Maritimes had long since been denuded for the British market – Nova Scotia did not have enough pine even for initial construction. New Brunswick and Quebec might manage for the first set of bridges, but would have difficulty when it came time to renew them. There were secondary costs associated with wooden bridges, the main one being that their average life was twelve years compared to iron, which was virtually indestructible. There was constant upkeep to wooden bridges and they were a fire hazard, which made watchmen necessary during the dry summer months. Fleming acknowledged that the initial cost of iron was greater, but he showed how expenses could be kept down by bringing in prefabricated bridge sections on ships as close as possible, then floating them the rest of the way.

Macdonald was loath to get caught in the middle of these disputes, and certainly did not care to overrule the important political interests represented on the board of commissioners; his one desire was to see construction get under way with the least possible delay. Accordingly, the board had its way on the tendering process and the first tenders for 144 kilometres were let – under the distance system – in February 1869. There was an enormous variation in the bids, one section varying from a low of $175,000 to a high of $700,000. In every case, the commissioners recommended accepting the lowest and, just as Fleming had predicted, by the end of the year many of the contractors were in difficulty and progress was lagging. Contractors sought urgent assistance from the board; instead, the commissioners annulled more than half the contracts, and re-let them. The board did not, however, rethink its contract policy even for a moment.

In their private reflections though, some of the commissioners must have wondered if Fleming was right, and on the bridge construction issue, they did accept that where river spans were especially long or high, iron would be more suitable. Fleming, however, was unyielding in his insistence on iron throughout the line and continued to appeal to the exasperated prime minister.

The aptly named Mr. Brydges, for his part, undertook to put the matter to rest once and for all in a paper he submitted to the government. He contended that Fleming's cost estimates for iron were simply wrong, that its use would delay completion of the line, and that the alleged fire hazards of wood had been greatly exaggerated; in his eighteen years as a railway manager, Brydges stated he had not heard of a single instance of a wooden bridge going up in flames. This provided Fleming with an easy opening; he observed that within a few weeks of Brydges' paper not one but two bridges on his own GTR had been destroyed by fire. The commissioners' arguments literally having gone up in smoke, they acknowledged defeat and recommended that all Intercolonial bridges of more than eighteen metres' span be of iron. This was still not good enough for Fleming, who persisted until at last, in May 1871, the government conceded the victory to him. Fleming's original estimate for all iron bridges was remarkably close to the final expense, which in the end was $20,000 less than estimated and, interestingly, less than if they had been of wood.

Never one to miss an opportunity to rake over old coals when it came to Fleming, Brydges was no less shy in seeking the main chance for his own Grand Trunk Railway. He wrote to Macdonald in December 1869:

> You have the command of large sums of money for the Intercolonial which are not wanted for immediate employment. It is as necessary for the future of Canada, that the Grand Trunk should be property maintained, as that the Intercolonial itself should be built and surely there can be no sound statesmanlike reason, why a reasonable loan on perfect security, should not be allowed in order to accomplish such indispensable results.[4]

Brydges was looking for a loan of £250,000 per year for three years to help bolster the GTR bonds which were at that time unsaleable in England at any price.

Once the intercolonial surveys were complete and the construction in full swing, Fleming's work was centred in Ottawa, where the major decisions were being made. It was his duty as chief engineer to oversee the work of the contractors and to report to the government on progress. He could scarcely do so from Halifax, and so in October 1869 Sandford and Jeanie turned the house in Halifax over to a housekeeper, farmed out the two cows, and moved to Ottawa with their children, governess, and cook. They did not, however, cut their ties with Halifax, and every summer they returned to holiday at their property on the North West Arm, travelling on the Intercolonial with a stopover along the way at a fishing camp Fleming leased on the Restigouche River.

Sandford and Jeanie moved into an imposing house, "Winterholme," at the corner of Daly and Chapel Streets in Ottawa. Life in Ottawa was very agreeable; they could more easily visit their families at Peterborough and Collingwood. In January 1871 Jeanie gave birth to a son, Hugh. They were firmly established in Ottawa's social swim. Fleming now had considerable means; shortly after taking up residence he and Jeanie gave a housewarming ball for 150 guests. Fleming was elected an officer of the Rideau Hall Curling Club, where he played regularly with the governor general and Ottawa's social elite. Sandford and Jeanie dined occasionally with Sir John and Lady Macdonald, although not surprisingly, perhaps, Macdonald seems not to have been overly fond of him; Fleming would never let an opportunity pass to bend the prime minister's ear in his interminable squabbles with the railway commissioners. Lady Macdonald, however, did enjoy their company, and Fleming was a special favourite of the Macdonalds' invalid daughter, Mary, who kept up an affectionate correspondence with him for years.

Fleming, for his part, had a much warmer relationship with Tupper. Thoroughly fed up with the constant battles with the commissioners, Fleming felt that Macdonald was not vigorous enough in taking his views into account. Privately, he would not have been sorry if, in the fluid political situation of the day, Macdonald were dislodged and replaced by Tupper. He wrote to Tupper in September 1869:

> When you reach Ottawa you will find the Government very strong, in my mind too strong, it will stand a fair chance before long of breaking in two, but how and when you will be better able to judge than I am. There is no opposition worthy of the name at present but you will find amongst conservatives and reformers from Ontario and perhaps other provinces an undercurrent of dissatisfaction. A good deal of it caused by Intercolonial Railway matters as you can imagine. With regard to this neither Govt nor Commrs have

appeared to take any notice of my last communication and I left on friendly terms with all of them ... Sir John I feel believes I am right, but everything is subordinate to political expediency with him. McDougall is the only other Minister I have talked freely to, he also fully agrees with me, but he will interfere as little as possible, for reasons you will under-stand. I do not believe my letters have been read with any care if at all by any of them and they will not be read until they are printed. I feel therefore (in the interest of the undertaking) that the sooner this is done the better. It might at all events have the effect of preventing the Commrs going any deeper into the mire.

I throw out these suggestions for your consideration. After a few days in Ottawa you will understand the whole position of affairs better than I do and will then know whether to act or remain passive as may seem best. I may say this much from what I have gathered, if at any time in the future you may see it expedient to strike out on an indepen-dent line you may safely calculate on winning a great many friends and supporters from Ontario. You have already a great many admirers in that quarter, mainly for your consis-tency and moderation. Do not however be at all in a hurry in any thing of this kind, make very sure of your ground. You have only had one session to cultivate it and that may be insufficient. [Tupper was now in the federal Parliament.]

You will I am sure pardon me for these hints knowing as you do so much better how and when to act than I possibly can. You will however give me credit for taking the deepest interest in your career, and hence the liberty I take. I am at the same time not mistaken in the belief that you feel inter-ested in the affairs in which I am engaged.[5]

The Intercolonial line was opened in stages as sections were completed; the section south of Moncton in 1873, the connection between Rivière du Loup and St. Flavie in August 1874, between Campbellton and Moncton in 1876. The entire line was operational by summer 1876 and the first through train from Halifax, carrying Tilley in a private car, arrived in Quebec City on 6 July. It was a remarkable achievement that had sorely taxed the resources of the young country. Construction of the Intercolonial had cost $36 million by the end of June 1878; gross revenues that year were $1.4 million and working expenses $1.6 million. By the year ending 30 June 1881 gross earnings slightly exceeded working expenses, putting paid to the argument that the Intercolonial would not pay its way for the foreseeable future.

Fleming's contribution to the railway's realization was a personal triumph, all the greater in the context of the persistent patronage and interference by the board of commissioners. The most remarkable feature of Fleming's achievement, however, is the fact that for the last five years of the Intercolonial project he was at the same time chief engineer of a transcontinental railway to the Pacific. Fleming's final report to Parliament on the Intercolonial was published in book form, and still stands as the best history available on the origins and construction of the railway.

CHAPTER 5

UNIVERSAL TIME

Fleming took a year's leave of absence from the railway department in 1876, and with Jeanie and the six children boarded the steamship *United Kingdom* at Quebec City in July. En route for Glasgow, the ship landed first at Londonderry, Ireland, and the two-day stopover allowed Fleming just enough time to visit a friend who lived at Sligo, far from the railway line. The travel arrangements were complicated, beginning with a train journey from Londonderry and continuing by coach. What followed, trivial in itself, would in due course alter the method of reckoning time all over the world. Looking forward to seeing his friend, Fleming consulted the Official Irish Travelling Guide and determined from it that he could catch a train en route to his destination at 5:35 p.m. Allowing plenty of time, he arrived at the train station with half an hour to spare, only to find the station platform deserted. The station-master referred Fleming to the bulletin board, which showed that the train was due at 5:35 a.m. and not 5:35 p.m. – the printed schedule was wrong. Fleming was obliged to cool his heels for the next twelve hours, eventually arriving at his friend's house sixteen and a half hours late.

The annoyance and frustration of the unnecessary delay planted the seed of an idea in Fleming's mind; surely, he thought, the solution to the confusing practice of showing time as a.m. and p.m. was as simple as replacing the system of two twelve-hour series with one of twenty-four consecutive hours. The idea was not entirely novel; it was practised by the Italians, Poles, and Bohemians. There was, however, a confusing array of time-reckoning systems in use around the world. The twenty-four-hour clock could not offer the solution unless it was universally accepted, and since the hours of darkness and light varied around the globe according to the earth's rotation, an arbitrary point of reference on earth would have to be selected as a zero point against which timepieces around the world would be set according to their distance from it; the several regions of the world would then be plus or minus so many hours from the zero point or prime meridian. The idea of a twenty-four-hour notation and adherence to a universal standard is taken for granted today but it was a matter of lively debate last century.

Fleming, of course, was particularly conscious of the special problems the prevailing uncoordinated systems of time reckoning posed for transportation. Those problems had already been addressed in England; when railways came into common use there, Greenwich Observatory time became the standard throughout the country. The situation was infinitely more complicated and confusing in North America, because of the vast distances involved.

While in London Fleming conducted research into the whole question of time reckoning, and put his observations on paper; in the winter of 1877–78 he circulated copies of his memoir to friends. Later, back in Canada, he rearranged and rewrote it as two papers for presentation to the Canadian Institute at its January and February 1879 meetings – "Time Reckoning" and "The Selection of a Prime Meridian to be Common to all Nations in Connection with Time Reckoning."

Fleming was amazed at the passive acceptance of the archaic and cumbersome practices of time reckoning. To him, it was natural and inevitable to take the large view of the matter, and proceed to set it right; with his restless. far-seeing imagination, he could not abide such an obviously antiquated and retrograde systems.

> Within a comparatively recent period, the human race has acquired control over a power, which has, in a remarkable degree, changed the conditions of human affairs. The application of steam to locomotion by land and water has given an enormous stimulus to progress throughout the world, and with the electric telegraph as an auxiliary, has somewhat rudely shaken customs and habits which have been handed down to us from bygone centuries. We still cling, however, to the system of Chronometry inherited from a remote antiquity, notwithstanding difficulties and inconveniences which are so familiar that they are not regarded, or are silently endured.[1]

In the 1870s every major community kept its own time, making for great confusion; the traveller who set out from Halifax to Toronto by train, his watch still set at Halifax time, found a different time kept at every stop along the way. Should he break his journey at St. John, Quebec City or Montreal, say, he would have to adjust his watch to local time. By the time the traveller arrived at Toronto he would have passed through five standards of time, and yet clocks at Toronto would be set only one hour and five minutes behind Halifax. The confusion in the United States with its many population centres was even greater. The situation was so absurd that some travellers carried watches with several faces to show the time in various centres. And as if that were not confusion enough, many cities observed more than one time standard – local time and railway time; in 1879 no fewer than seventy-five distinct local time standards were used by American railways, all different, the greatest difference reaching 3 hours 58 minutes.

In the interest of correcting this chaotic situation, Fleming proposed an entirely new approach to standardized time reckoning. First, time notation would be based on a solar day divided into twenty-four equal parts; communities could keep local time if they wished, but there must be a universally applied and consistent means of harmonizing local times around the world. Fleming designated the twenty-four divisions by letters of the alphabet along equally spaced lines of longitude on a globe, the letter A at the starting point or prime meridian. Because of the rivalry that inevitably would arise over the selection of the prime meridian, Fleming suggested it be fixed 180 degrees from the Greenwich meridian, where it would touch no continent except the eastern extremity of the north of Asia which was sparsely populated. He had no strong views, however, on where the meridian might be, whether Yokohama, Cairo, St. Petersburg, Greenwich or Washington, so long as timekeepers everywhere set their clocks in accordance with the universal standard. Each timepiece would show local time, and the time anywhere in the world, at a glance.

While Fleming's thoughts on timekeeping were original, he was not alone in pondering the problem. The American Metrological Society had set up a standard time committee in 1874 to consider harmonizing the time reckoning across the United States; the committee's president, Prof. Cleveland Abbe of the United States Signal Office, by pure coincidence also proposed a twenty-four-hour clock to the society in 1878. In another paper at the same meeting Frederick Brooks revived an old idea that had first surfaced in the aftermath of the French Revolution – a decimal day of twenty units instead of twenty-four hours, further divided into forty parts. The Standard Time Committee took up the various proposals and in May 1879 reported to the society, which in turn resolved that local time should be discontinued and all public institutions regulate clocks by the standard adopted by the principal railroads in their respective localities. The society further recommended there not be more than one standard of time for every hour of longitude west of the Greenwich meridian.

Meanwhile, and quite independently, the Canadian Institute became excited by Fleming's imaginative papers on time reckoning, and decided to take up the campaign for time reform; the institute called on the governor general to bring Fleming's proposals to the attention of the imperial government so that it might, in turn, bring them to the notice of scientific authorities around the world. And so Fleming's universal standard time began to attract wider notice, not all of it positive. The astronomer royal at Greenwich, Sir G.B. Airy, was unimpressed: "I set not the slightest value on the remarks extending through the early part of Mr. Fleming's paper. Secondly as to the need of a Prime Meridian no practical man ever wants such a thing." Not wanting to close his options however, "If a Prime Meridian were to be adopted, it must be that of Greenwich, for the navigation of almost the whole world depends on calculations founded on that of Greenwich."[2]

The astronomer royal for Scotland liked Fleming's scheme even less.

> Mr. Sandford Fleming seems to know perfectly well that in making such a proposition he is running full tilt against common sense and universal experience. But then he urges the plea of national jealousies being aroused if the Prime Meridian were to pass through the country of one powerful European nation more conveniently for its inhabitants that for those of another; so he does them all equally a mischief by making his Meridian convenient to no one; and proudly holds that the grand object now of advanced civilization is to consult in everything the utmost development of internationality, or the breaking down of all the ancient bounds which have hitherto divided one nation from another, and in fact formed them into nations![3]

The Royal Society of England was more positive; the society secretary wrote to the Canadian governor general:

> The convenience of a system of time reckoning, which should be common to all the earth, is easily seen, while at the same time it is obvious that if such a reckoning be at all generally used, there must be a means of readily passing from it to local time, which is ultimately bound up with the daily business of life. The means recommended by the author, are simple and seem well devised. The difficulty is of course, to induce the different civilized nations of the world to concur in this, or any similar scheme.[4]

The society favoured Fleming's suggestion of a prime meridian through the Pacific Ocean.

Other institutions commented favourably on Fleming's proposals – the Spanish Navy liked them, and so did the Imperial Academy of Science at

St. Petersburg. Fleming was invited to present a paper on his universal standard time proposals to the American Society of Civil Engineers' convention in Montreal in June 1881. Fleming proposed that North America lead the way for the rest of the world with five meridians, exactly one hour apart, with the middle one six hours west of Greenwich, and passing almost directly through the city of New Orleans. After discussion, Fleming's paper was referred by the society to a special committee, to be chaired by Fleming, with representatives of American railroads and experts in civil engineering, for further consideration.

Fleming's time proposals became a catalyst for closer contacts between scientific institutions in Canada, the United States, and Europe, and in the process played a part in expanding Canada's international presence. The Canadian Institute and the American Metrological Society joined hands to set up a combined committee on uniform standard time, and decided to send a joint delegation to the International Geographical Congress at Venice, Italy in September 1881; the Canadian team included Fleming, the Canadian Institute's president, John Langton, and the president of the University of Toronto, Daniel Wilson.

Fleming travelled to Venice with his twenty-two-year-old daughter, Minnie. They left Halifax in August aboard the Intercolonial; at Rimouski they caught the *Sardinian* for Liverpool, England. In London Fleming was startled by a slap on the back as he was looking in a shop window in Piccadilly; turning about he found himself face to face with Sir John A. Macdonald who as it turned out was, by sheer coincidence, staying at the same hotel. Fleming, Minnie, Sir John, and Lady Macdonald went shopping together and took a coach trip into the countryside. Fleming and Minnie left London on 7 September for the Continent, travelling to Italy by way of Holland, Germany, and Austria.

The International Geographical Congress was opened by Italy's King and Queen in the splendour of the ancient Doge's Palace in Venice on 15 September. Six days later Fleming read his paper on the adoption of a prime meridian. He submitted seven resolutions to the congress:

- That the unification of initial meridians of reference for computing longitude is of great importance in the interests of geography and navigation;
- That the selection of a zero-meridian for the world would greatly promote the cause of general uniformity and exactness in time reckoning;
- That in the interests of all mankind it is eminently desirable that civilized nations should come to an agree-

ment with respect to the determination of a common prime meridian, and a system of universal time reckoning;

- That the Governments of different countries be appealed to immediately after the close of Congress, with the view of ascertaining if they would be disposed to assist in the matter by nominating persons to confer with each other and endeavour to reach a conclusion which they would recommend their respective governments to adopt;

- That in view of the representations which have come to this Congress from America, it is suggested that a Conference of Delegates who may be appointed by the different governments be held in the city of Washington and that the Conference open on the first Monday in May, 1882;

- That the gentlemen whose names follow be in Executive Committee to make arrangements for the proposed Meeting of Delegates, and to take such steps as may seem expedient in furtherance of the objects of these Resolutions and that all communications in respect thereof be transmitted to General W.B. Hazen, Metrological Bureau, War Department, Washington;

- That the Italian Government be respectfully requested to communicate these resolutions to the Governments of all other countries.

The resolutions were adopted, but the Italians were slow to issue invitations to a meeting hosted by the Americans, and for the time being nothing further was done. The American Metrological Society took matters into its own hands in December and approached the American president and Congress to suggest they call an international conference in Washington to promote universal standard time.

The American Society of Civil Engineers met in Washington in May 1882, and considered the report of its special committee on uniform time it had set up at the Montreal convention. In the interim, the committee had issued a questionnaire to a wide cross-section of informed people in the United States, Canada, and Mexico with such questions as: "Do you consider it desirable to have a system of uniform standard time for North America?" and "Do you favour a system of uniform time throughout the world?" The committee reported a remarkable unanimity of view in North America in favour of standard time; 100 percent support for a system for North America and 95 percent for a world system. The committee accordingly recommended that the countries of North America not wait for other countries, but proceed right away to adopt a system capable of extension to the whole globe. The recommendations of the committee were adopted by the convention, and a resolution was passed calling on the United States Congress to take the necessary steps to have a prime meridian established. With pressure mounting from different directions, Congress acceded in August 1882, and voted to hold an international conference to settle the matter once and for all.

This posed a problem for Canada, which strictly speaking had no diplomatic relations of its own with the United States so long as the imperial government remained responsible for its external relations. And yet Canada, through the impetus of Fleming, was the leader of the movement for universal standard time, and was seen as such by the international community. The Royal Society of Canada petitioned the governor general in January 1883 to take steps to have Canada represented at the Washington Conference; he had eighteen months to sort it out. Meanwhile, in October 1883, representatives of American railroads met to consider a way out of the intolerable confusion reigning in their industry because of several score time standards across the country. They agreed to implement Fleming's scheme for North America and, on November 18, standard time went into effect on the railways, with many communities following suit.

Delegates from twenty-five countries met in Washington in October 1884 for the opening of the International Prime Meridian Conference. The four-man United Kingdom delegation included representatives of the Royal Navy, the Cambridge Observatory, the Council of India, and, in the person of Sandford Fleming, Canada. Fleming had prepared twenty-four recommendations for the conference on the regulation of time, the reckoning of longitude, and the adoption of a prime meridian. The last was the most contentious issue, because countries were reluctant to reset their clocks to accord with a prime meridian in a country other than their own. Some, including Fleming, favoured a meridian running along the Bering Strait, 180 degrees from Greenwich; others favoured Greenwich because of its established use in England; still others favoured a meridian in line with the Great Pyramid at Giza, Egypt, since it was a universally recognized landmark and its geographical situation was central to the so-called civilized world. After much debate, the Conference concluded a month later with a unanimous vote in favour of establishment of a prime meridian; and selection of Greenwich as the prime meridian was passed by twenty-two votes to one (San Domingo against) with two abstentions (Brazil and France).

For Fleming, it was the triumphant realization of the dream that began on a deserted railway station platform in Ireland eight years before. Universal Standard Time went into effect at Greenwich on 1 January 1885, and in March the colonial secretary conveyed to Fleming the appreciation of the imperial government for his services at the Washington Conference. Many years would pass before the new time system was accepted around the world; France was one of the most recalcitrant holdouts, even though Paris time was only a few minutes off Greenwich Mean Time.

Fleming would not be satisfied until the universal system became truly universal; he continued to promote it through speeches, articles, and correspondence for years to come. The special committee on Universal Standard Time of the American Society of Civil Engineers, chaired by Fleming, continued to meet to discuss progress, and to present an annual report on attempts to persuade governments to implement the system. North America's adoption of the system with a minimum of fuss or inconvenience proved it could be done without hardship, and it set a model that was followed over time by one country after another all over the world.

On 10 June 1886, two weeks before the first regularly scheduled train for the Pacific coast steamed out of Montreal, the vice-president of the Canadian Pacific Railway Company, William Van Horne, issued the following circular:

> In view of the new conditions that have to be met by this Company in establishing a continuous train service on a line of Railway covering 55 degrees of longitude and soon to cover 60 degrees (or four hours of time), it is necessary for convenience and to avoid confusion, to adopt what is known as the "24 hour system," that is, to substitute the numbers 13 to 24 for the present pm hours 1 to 12, so that the hours from midnight will be numbered from 1 to 24.
>
> A large majority of the Railway Managers of Canada and the United States have formally expressed their opinion in favour of the "24 hour" system, and this opinion is concurred in by the public press and by all the leading scientific men of the continent.
>
> The wisdom of the adoption of the "Standard Time" system which is now used throughout North America is no longer disputed, and it is only a question of a very short time when the "24 hour" system will be as generally followed. It will be an honour to Canada to take the lead in this important reform. The Directors in taking this step hope for the approval of the Public and the hearty cooperation of all the Employees of the Company. It is

intended to make the change first on all lines of the Company west of Lake Superior, beginning with the next change in time-tables.

Paper dials with the new afternoon numbers will be furnished both for clocks and watches free of charge to the public as well as to employees of the Company. These dials may be easily applied to any watch or clock by following the directions accompanying this circular. Arrangements will be made at the different divisional points for their application to the watches of employees and those who are unable to have them applied by the persons appointed for the purpose may obtain them from any agent of the Company. Those requiring dials for clocks should state the diameter of the clock dials inside of the present figures.[5]

CHAPTER 6

LOOKING WEST

It was at a town hall meeting in Port Hope, Ontario, in 1858 that Fleming first advanced his vision of a railway line spanning the North American continent, entirely within British territory. The idea itself had been contemplated long before; in the 1840s and 1850s several visionaries had forecast a rail, or a part-rail, part-water route to the Pacific. Nova Scotia's Joseph Howe predicted in 1851 that, sooner or later, the whistle of the steam engine would be heard in the Rocky Mountains; in the same year, Allan Macdonnell of Toronto sought a charter from the Canadian assembly for a "Lake Superior and Pacific Railroad Company," to build a line from Lake Superior to Burrard Inlet on the Pacific coast. Macdonnell's scheme was doomed to go nowhere, however, so long as the Hudson's Bay Company controlled the vast territories of the Northwest. A separate effort by A.N. Morin in 1854 to incorporate a "Northern Pacific Railway Company" was no more successful, but it was now only a matter of time before the Hudson's Bay Company stranglehold would be broken.

The imperial government, in partnership with the Royal Geographic Society, in 1857 despatched an expedition, led by Captain Palliser, to gather information on a western route favourable for emigration, to ascertain the nature of the country west of Red River and the elbow of the Saskatchewan, and to find a pass or passes across the Rocky Mountains. The reports of Palliser's monumental three-year expedition told of the vast agricultural and mining potential of the Northwest, but advised against the building of a railway entirely through British America to the Pacific. Palliser wrote:

> ... knowledge of the country, on the whole, would never lead me to advocate a line of communication from Canada across the continent to the Pacific, exclusively through British territory. The time has now for ever isolated the Central American possessions of Great Britain from Canada in the east, and almost debarred them from any eligible access from the Pacific coast on the west.[1]

Meanwhile, even as Palliser was trekking across the central plains, others were promoting their separate dreams of a transcontinental railway; the "North-West Transportation, Navigation and Railway Company" was incorporated in 1858 but never got off the ground.

The Province of Canada decided to launch two expeditions of its own, similar to Palliser's – one led by George Gladman and the other by Henry Youle Hind; unlike Palliser, both Gladman and Hind concluded that a railway route entirely across British territory was a practical proposition. Hind was accompanied on his expedition by Sandford Fleming's youngest brother, John, who was a provincial land surveyor. John Fleming was even more talented than his brother in drawing, and his sketches and watercolours of the prairies were widely acclaimed; his own explorations were included in Hind's report for 1859. Between 1863 and 1870 John Fleming was engaged in surveys on the Northern Railway, and Sandford employed him on the preliminary Intercolonial survey in 1863–64. John's health suffered, however, from the rigours of his prairie explorations, and he was unable to continue survey work after 1874.

Hind published his "Overland Route to British Columbia" in 1862, supporting his case for a railway with a paper written by Sandford Fleming, "Practical Observations on the Construction of a Continuous Line of Railway from Canada to the Pacific Ocean on British Territory." It was this widely publicized report that commended Fleming to the Red River colonists.

These early western explorations excited great interest, throughout British America and abroad, in the enormous potential of the Northwest for farming and settlement. And at the same time, the right set of circumstances was conspiring to make railway talk a more practical proposition – the discovery of gold in British Columbia attracted prospectors to the colony in droves; political unity was being forged in the east; there was growing apprehension of American intent once the Civil War was over; and with the American Midwest rapidly filling up with settlers, the empty lands to the north looked more attractive. Most important of all, the days of Hudson's Bay Company control over the Northwest were numbered.

Alfred Waddington, an engineer, was attracted to British Columbia by the Cariboo country gold boom; he became interested in prospects for improved transportation to get to the mining areas inland, and sank a personal fortune in an attempt to build a road from Bute Inlet on the Pacific Coast to the Cariboo; but persistent conflicts with the local aboriginal people forced him to abandon the project in 1864. With increasing talk of British Columbia entering the Canadian Confederation, however, Waddington widened his horizons to think in terms of a railway, and in 1868 read a paper before the Royal Geographic Society, putting his case for a transcontinental railway from Bute Inlet through the Rockies by way of Yellowhead Pass (so named for a blond-haired Métis in the area) to Edmonton and the Red River.

Not everyone rejoiced in the vision of a Canada extending westward to the Pacific shore, certainly not the member of Parliament for Leeds and Grenville North, Francis Jones, who opposed the Intercolonial. According to Jones, the existing Dominion was territory enough, considering that half that amount in Europe supported fifty million inhabitants.

The Hudson's Bay Company ceded control of the Northwest to Canada in December 1869; the Métis population was incensed by the lack of consultation and saw its interests and way of life sold down the river. The ensuing rebellion, led by the Métis leader, Louis Riel, alerted the federal government to the security needs of the west; a railway line would have permitted the quick despatch of troops to the front lines before matters got out of hand. There was also a well-founded fear of American designs on the Northwest in the wake of the Métis uprising. C.J. Brydges wrote to John A. Macdonald in January to report on a meeting with Governor Smith of Vermont concerning railway business – Smith, who was also president of the Northern Pacific Railway, told Brydges of the work in progress to extend his line from Lake Superior to the Red River within the United States, and then northwest, all of it running between 32 and 48 kilometres from the Canadian border. According to Brydges:

> He made no secret further of the fact, that in his arrangements, they were working in concert with certain parties at Washington – meaning, I presume, the Government – that they hope to carry the line so near the boundary, that drop lines into the territory may be constructed, and thus injure, if not prevent, the construction of an independent line in British territory.
>
> There is no doubt whatever, from what he tells me, that the Government are assisting the Northern Pacific Company to go on with their work, in the hope that it will have an effect in maintaining the present attitude of Riel and his party.
>
> Governor Smith is counting upon some more material aid from the Government, so as to ensure a speedy prosecution of the works.
>
> I am quite satisfied from the way Smith talks to me, that there is some political action at the bottom of this, and that the United States Government at Washington are anxious to take advantage of the organization of this Northern

Pacific Railway to prevent your getting the control for Canada of the Hudson's Bay Territory ... It seems to me you ought carefully to consider what had better be done, as, no doubt, the Minnesota people are letting the insurgents in Red River understand that their only hope of getting railway communication will be through United States sources.[2]

Macdonald replied to Brydges:

It is quite evident to me ... from advices from Washington, that the United States Government are resolved to do all they can, short of war, to get possession of the western territory and we must take immediate and vigorous steps to counteract them. One of the first things to be done is to show unmistakably our resolve to build the Pacific Railway. As I have already talked over this subject fully with you, I need not go into it again. It must be taken up by a body of capitalists, and not constructed by the Government directly. Canada can promise more liberal grants of land in alternate blocks, and may perhaps (but of this I cannot speak with any confidence) induce Parliament to add a small pecuniary subsidy. No time should be lost in this, and I should think that we had made a great stride if we got you to take it up vigorously ... The thing must not be allowed to sleep, and I want you to address yourself to it at once and work out a plan. Cartier and I will talk it over, after conference with you, and push it through.[3]

The province of Manitoba was carved out of the government's newly acquired western territories in 1870. Well before that, the British Columbians had been ready to make a deal to join Canada – the heady days of the gold rush had declined since 1863, and with the American purchase of Alaska from the Russians in 1867, the colony was hemmed in on two sides. With the Rocky Mountain barrier to the east, and the Pacific Ocean on the west, a nervous British Columbia cast its lot for Canada and passed a resolution in 1867 calling for federation with the new Dominion. Now that the federal government had title to the Northwest, the incorporation of the Pacific colony seemed sensible and practicable. Terms were negotiated and one of the conditions was a federal commitment to begin construction, within two years, of a railway to connect the seaboard of British Columbia with the railway system of Canada, and to finish the job within ten years.

An enormous task lay before the country – three and a half million people, concentrated almost entirely in the east, had undertaken to build a transcontinental railway several thousand kilometres long, across vast stretches of granite and dense forest cover north of Lake Superior, and muskeg swamps, treeless plains, and nearly impenetrable mountain ranges in the west. Little was known yet about the precise location of lakes and rivers, or the particular properties of the terrain, but if the engineering challenges were daunting, the financial requirements were staggering; it would cost an estimated $100 million, approximately $30 for every man, woman and child in Canada, an extraordinary sum in those days.

In March 1871, the government authorized a survey to be conducted in four sections: between the Ottawa Valley and the Nipigon, from Nipigon to Fort Garry, from Fort Garry to the Rocky Mountains, and from the Rocky Mountains to the Pacific Coast. Macdonald wanted Francis Shanly to be chief engineer for the Pacific railway project, but his public works minister, Hector Langevin, put forward Sandford Fleming's name on the understanding he would be relieved of his Intercolonial duties. Macdonald acquiesced, but as it turned out, no successor for the Intercolonial was found; Fleming was assured that he would receive good support while keeping the responsibility for both enormous jobs. Fleming got the support he wanted with the appointment of J.H. Rowan from the Public Works Department as his chief assistant, while Collingwood Schreiber became the effective head of Intercolonial construction.

Fleming believed from the very beginning that the Pacific railway should be built by private enterprise, with strong backing from the government; his experience of the Intercolonial running through the empty and still unproductive spaces of New Brunswick convinced him of this. He cautioned, as well, against proceeding too fast with construction, thinking it best to allow the line to proceed in step with settlement to sustain it; the government did not want to hear of this, however, in view of its commitment to British Columbia to begin construction within two years, and have it completed within ten.

In the months before British Columbia's effective date of union with Canada, Fleming and his deputy, Rowan, set about to assemble a staff and compile a digest of all known information about the lands between Ontario and the Pacific; from this they set a work plan for surveys. It was difficult to assemble a competent staff, however, with so many experienced men at work on the Intercolonial, and so many incompetent political appointees – the curse of government-led projects. Rowan set out with thirteen parties of surveyors in June 1870 to position them at various points between the Ottawa Valley and the Red River; each party was assigned 120 kilometres per season. John Trutch, R. McLennan, and Walter Moberly were appointed to examine the terrain between the Rocky Mountains and the Pacific.

Fleming split the survey into three regions – Lake Superior to the prairies, the prairies to the mountains, and the mountains to the Pacific – with twenty-one smaller divisions, each supervised by an assistant engineer reporting directly to Fleming, based in Ottawa. Survey parties numbered about forty men – four or five engineers, assisted by trail blazers, packmen, a cook, and a commissariat officer. Eight hundred men were in the field in the first season with work beginning the day British Columbia entered Confederation. Fleming decided that to expedite the work the number of exploratory surveys would be kept to a minimum; planning would depend instead on the information already known about the general route. On that basis, a full-scale instrumental survey was begun right away. This decision would become a matter of enormous controversy later on.

An elaborate supply system was created to keep the field crews in food and equipment, but there were many hitches, and when supplies did not arrive in the right place at the right time there was hardship. The field crews suffered greatly – plagued by mosquitoes and black flies and in constant danger from forest and prairie grass fires, and flash floods. They had to endure bitter cold in the mountain passes and sweltered in the summer sun on the treeless plains as they tested the soil, checked the altitude and mileage, and measured the bends. Twelve men died from drowning alone in the 1872 survey season. The pay was meagre compensation – engineers in charge of survey parties received $160 per month, packers $50 to $90, and axemen $40; all were provisioned at the government's expense. Sometimes the loneliness, hunger, and fatigue in the field became too much to bear, and crews rebelled against the engineers. Fleming posted a steady stream of correspondence to the government, pleading for better support for his men, but he was in no hurry to complete the surveys to make way for the construction crews; he wrote to the Public Works Department in April 1872 that as thorough an examination of the country as possible should be made before beginning construction; to do otherwise could result in costly blunders. The Public Works Department, on the other hand, cast a wary eye on the rapidly escalating costs, and on the calendar.

First reports from the field parties arrived in Fleming's office in early 1872. Moberly's preliminary examination of the Yellowhead and Howse passes through the Rockies satisfied Fleming that the Howse should be dismissed, and accordingly, the Yellowhead was confirmed by the government in April. Fleming's first annual report to the government already indicated the general course of the line; and with the route for the railway more or less understood, Fleming undertook to check it for himself, as he had done on the Intercolonial. He invited two good friends from Halifax, the clergyman George Grant and Dr. Arthur Moren, to meet him in Toronto in July for an expedition to the Pacific coast. Fleming also sent a message to Moberly in British Columbia, instructing him to abandon his surveys of the Howse Pass and meet him in the Yellowhead in late summer. Fleming, his son Franky, Grant, Moren, Colonel Robertson Ross (adjutant general of the militia) and his son Hugh set off from Toronto in July, by train, for Collingwood with the expedition cook, Sergeant Terry McWilliams. The colonel and his son would stay with the party on the first leg, as far as Fort Garry. Grant became secretary to the expedition, and his daily account of the trek to the Pacific later was published as a book, *Ocean to Ocean*. Somewhat embarrassingly, it emerged eventually that Fleming had personally advanced $2,000 of public funds to the printer for publication of Grant's book. Fleming argued before a parliamentary public accounts committee that he considered it important to disseminate information about the largely unknown western region to the widest audience – if the proceeds from the sale of the book were not sufficient, he was prepared to reimburse the public purse himself. In fact all five thousand copies were sold, and all expenses paid.

Grant wrote up his daily account at the campsite each night, usually in a notebook but sometimes on strips of birch bark. His published diary excited the public's imagination – here was an account of one of the greatest overland treks in Canadian history, undertaken by railway, lake steamer, Red River cart, canoe, horseback and on foot. Grant vividly portrayed the tremendous potential of the west in agriculture, mining, and settlement; against this he weighed the rigours of harsh winters, deep frosts, plagues of locusts and drought – but the vision of the west as a region of great bounty was unmistakable.

The expedition began on the Northern Railway to Collingwood, where they boarded a steamer for Lake Superior and Thunder Bay. Fleming noticed among the passengers a peculiar but enthusiastic man on a botanical holiday; wherever the steamer docked the man was always first ashore, scooping up samples of mosses, ferns, grasses, and flowers. So extraordinary was his behaviour that he was nicknamed "the haypicker." John Macoun, forty years old, was professor of botany and geology at Albert College in Belleville, Ontario; quite clearly, he would be a great asset to Fleming's expedition, and was enlisted.

Fleming had devoted considerable time to the problems of isolation and loneliness for his far-flung survey crews; for example, he was mindful that most of them usually found themselves far from a church. A great respecter of Sunday worship, he undertook to provide his men with an alternative to church attendance, and after consultation with clergy from different denominations, compiled an inter – denominational prayer service, had it printed in pamphlet form and distributed among the survey parties. It was pressed into use aboard the steamer, with Grant officiating. Fleming's prayer sheets became popular over the years, and were the inspiration for some of Canada's earliest ecumenical services.

The steamer arrived at Prince Arthur's Landing, Thunder Bay, on 22 July, and the expedition's baggage was transferred to a heavy wagon. They travelled the seventy-two kilometres to Shebadowan where they transferred to canoes for the next 608 kilometres along the chain of lakes to Fort Garry, joined now by several Indian guides and oarsmen. The larger lakes were plied by steamtugs to which the Indians hooked on the canoes for a tow. Although Fleming's crew had some initial apprehensions about their travelling companions, they got on well with them.

> It never seemed to our Ojibbeways to wash, crop, or dress their hair. They let it grow, at its own sweet will, all around their faces and down their necks, lank, straight and stiff, helping the growth with fish oil; whereas, everyone of the Iroquois had "a good head of hair", thick, well cropped, and, though always black, quite like the hair of a civilized man instead of a savage. Our Ojibbeways had silver rings on their fingers, broad gaudy sashes and bedraggled feathers bound round their felt hats. The Iroquois dressed as simply and neatly as blue jackets.[4]

In the context of his time, Grant was sympathetic to the aboriginals, and the dislocation of their traditional life-style that railway construction inevitably would cause.

> And now a foreign race is swarming over the country, to mark out lines, to erect fences, and to say "this is mine and not yours," till not an inch shall be left the original owner. All this may be inevitable. But in the name of justice, of doing as we would be done by, of the "sacred rights" of property, is not the Indian entitled to liberal, and, if possible, permanent compensation?[5]

The party cleared the rapids and portages of the lakes, admiring the scenery and the good stands of timber along the way. Fleming recognized the potential of these forests as a bountiful source of sleepers for the railway bed across the treeless plains ahead; the logs could be cut at the water's edge, formed into rafts and floated to Winnipeg. Nearing Fort Garry, the nature of the country changed and became much flatter and more marshy. The expedition transferred to wagons again and proceeded west along the old Dawson road. Macoun was in seventh heaven among a seemingly inexhaustible array of new plants and grasses.

Fleming led his party into the village of Winnipeg and on to Fort Garry and the Government House – Winnipeg was wild west frontier.

> The drunkenness of Winnipeg is notorious; the clergy do all in their power, by precept and example, to check it, but they accomplish little. The Roman Catholic Bishop and his priests, all the Presbyterian and the Methodist Ministers, the Episcopal Archdeacon and several of his clergy are tee-totallers; but the "saloons" of Winnipeg are stronger than the Churches.[6]

The expedition parted company with Colonel Ross and his son at Fort Garry, and was joined by Charles Horetzky. Horetzky had formerly served with the Hudson's Bay Company, and knew the west well – he was also one of the best early photographers of the western plains. Like so many others of Fleming's staff, Horetzky got his job through political connections – in his case Charles Tupper.

Outside Fort Garry, Fleming's party was also joined by a Mr. McDougal, superintendent of the Wesleyan missions on the Saskatchewan, travelling with his Cree servant to his mission at Fort Victoria near Edmonton. The expedition continued westward with six Red River carts loaded with tents, baggage, and supplies; three drivers, two buckboards, saddle horses for everyone and eighteen extra horses. The pace was intense; they travelled four hundred kilometres a week across the Prairies. Ninety-six kilometres outside Fort Garry, along the Assiniboine River, the expedition came upon Silver Heights, the residence of the governor in America of the Hudson's Bay Company, Donald A. Smith.

Smith had come to Canada at the age of seventeen and began as a clerk for the Hudson's Bay Company in Labrador. He invested in the Bank of Montreal, and in due course became one of its largest shareholders. Smith eventually became governor of the Hudson's Bay Company and held sway over a region extending from Hudson Bay to the foot of the Rockies. He purchased all the Hudson's Bay Company stock offered when the Canadian government took over the Northwest, and came into control of the company. He was elected to Parliament in 1871. Smith entertained Fleming and his men to dinner, and equipped them for the onward journey; he and Fleming were to become fast friends.

From Manitoba, Fleming's party made for Fort Carlton on the North Saskatchewan River via Fort Ellice, the Qu'appelle Valley, Assiniboine River, and the South Saskatchewan. All along the way they passed rich, unexploited farmland, stands of trees, lakes, and ever new botanical species for Macoun. Two Hudson's Bay Company officers joined the party at Fort Carlton as far as Edmonton, together with two Métis and an Indian. The staple diet at this stage consisted largely of pemmican, prepared in as many different ways as the expedition's cook could dream up; sometimes a pike or whitefish was pulled from a lake, or a grouse shot for supper. At the forts along the way fresh buffalo steaks and potatoes were available. The party arrived at Edmonton on 27 August; this was the headquarters for the Hudson's Bay Company on the Saskatchewan. They spotted a coal seam jutting from the river bank; the place was not only a cornucopia of nature's riches but also the crossroads between the Prairies just crossed and the Rocky Mountains ahead. Fleming asked Horetzky and Macoun to proceed in a more northerly direction to the Peace River country to examine the terrain, and explore the northern passes through the Rockies, while the remainder proceeded in a more southerly direction to the Athabasca River and Jasper House. Leaving the carts behind for the ascent into the mountains, they loaded pack horses with the absolute minimum – no more than forty-eight kilograms per horse, including food for thirty days. There was no room for heavy tents; the men would sleep under lean-to's fashioned from a few poles and a cotton sheet or bits of birch bark, with a fire for warmth.

At night, temperatures dropped to freezing, and progress grew ever slower and more difficult as Fleming and his men climbed higher. They were joined on 14 September by Fleming's assistant surveyor for British Columbia, Walter Moberly, who was supervising survey parties in the Columbia River and Yellowhead Pass region. Moberly knew these mountains; he had come to British Columbia fifteen years before during the height of the gold rush. His preferred passage through the mountains was the Eagle Pass and onward to Burrard Inlet by way of the Columbia Valley and Fraser River. Competing interests in favour of one route or another were to become a tremendous contest in the engineering department, ultimately spelling trouble for the government.

Fleming and his party reached the summit of Yellowhead Pass on 16 September, and continued down the western slope. Grant recorded a welcome find:

> We crossed the Thompson at a point where it divides into three, the smallest of the three sections being bridged with long logs, the two others, broad and only 'belly deep', as Jack (an Indian guide) phrased it. Riding down the west side, too wet and tired to notice anything, the men in

advance passed a blazed tree with a piece of paper pinned to the blaze; but the Secretary, being on foot, turned aside to look; and read – 'In V's Cache there is a box for S. Fleming or Mr. Smith.' He at once called out the good news, and V's Cache in the shape of a small log shanty was found hard by. Jack unroofed it in a trice and jumped in; and among other things, stored for different engineering parties, was the 'box'. A stone broke it open, and as Jack handed out the contents, one by one, a general shout announced their nature – Candles and canned meat; good. 'Hooray' from the rear! Two bottles of Worcester sauce and a bottle of brandy! Better; sauce both for the fat pork and for the plum-pudding next Sunday. Half a dozen of Bass Pale Ale, with the familiar face of the red pyramid brand! Three times three and one cheer more! After this crowning mercy, more canned meats, jams and a few bottles of claret evoked but faint applause. The wine and jams were put back again for Mr. Smith. Four bottles of the ale, a can of the preserved beef, and another of peaches were opened on the spot, and Terry producing bread from the kitchen sack, an impromptu lunch was eaten round the Cache, and V's health drunk as enthusiastically as if he had been the greatest benefactor of his species.[7]

A week after clearing the Yellowhead, the party met with Marcus Smith on the Fraser River. Smith too had his favourite route through the mountains, farther north – the Pine Pass, across the Chilcotin Plains and through the Cascade Mountains to Bute Inlet on the Pacific coast. Fleming prevailed on Smith to set aside his explorations for the season, and accompany the party the rest of the way to Kamloops. They arrived there on 30 September, and at Burrard Inlet on 5 October, one week short of three months since setting out from Toronto. After visiting Victoria the party made arrangements to return home via San Francisco, and the railway across the United States.

CHAPTER 7

STORM CLOUDS

Powerful interests vied for the lucrative Pacific railway construction contract; the successful bidder would receive $30 million and 20.2 million hectares of land, in alternate blocks 32 kilometres deep on either side of the line (the other blocks to be sold by the government to recoup the cash payment). There would be a branch line from the Red River settlement to the United States border, and another from the main route across Northern Ontario to a point on the eastern end of Lake Superior. The Grand Trunk general manager Charles Brydges had the early running, thanks to his friend John A. Macdonald, but he failed to sway the government towards his own plan for a Pacific railway and dropped from the race. The field was left to two rival syndicates: the one headed by David L. Macpherson, the other by Sir Hugh Allan.

Once again, both men were friends of Macdonald, but Macpherson was closer; during the previous winter he had collected a $60,000 testimonial fund to help the prime minister out from under a crushing load of debts. An original sponsor of the Grand Trunk, Macpherson headed a Toronto group to form the Inter-Oceanic Railway Company to bid for the contract. Sir Hugh Allan from Montreal was head of the leading steamship service between Canada and Britain; he was also involved in banking, insurance, textiles, coal, and the major Canadian telegraph company, and had connections with the Northern Pacific Railway interests in the United States. Now he formed the Canada Pacific Railway Company; Donald Smith was a charter member, and on the board of directors. Brydges, however, refused to associate himself with Allan's company.

Macdonald wanted badly to get Macpherson and Allan to join forces, and together build the Pacific railway. Allan, however, insisted on the presidency of the proposed company and a controlling share of the stock for himself and his associates; Macpherson was equally insistent that the presidency and vice-presidency should be left an open question. With negotiations at an impasse Macdonald tried a different tack. A new charter was drawn up in February 1873, the preamble of which referred to the failure to amalgamate the two companies, considered it inadvisable to agree with either, and therefore incorporated a new company. In fact the new Canadian Pacific Railway Company included men from both of the previous ones – Hugh Allan assumed the presidency, and there were also A.G. Archibald from Halifax,

F.W. Cumberland of Toronto, Francis Shanly, and Sandford Fleming. The CPR Company was to have $10 million capital; representatives of the company set sail for Britain in March in search of financial backing.

A storm cloud, however, loomed menacingly over the CPR and the government. A Montreal businessman, Lucius Huntington, told the House of Commons in April that he could prove a deal had been struck between Allan and a Mr. G.W. McMullen, representing certain American capitalists, whereby the latter would provide the capital for construction of the Pacific railway, although it would present a false appearance as a purely Canadian company. Huntington further alleged that the government was aware of this and had agreed with Allan and his lawyer, J.J. Abbott, that Allan should advance a large sum of money to support the election of Conservative ministers and their supporters in the 1872 general election. In return, Allan would get the Pacific railway construction contract. A seriously embarrassed government appointed a committee to consider the charges, and in August the beleaguered Macdonald set up a full royal commission of inquiry. It was discovered that, in all, $350,000 had been advanced by Allan to Macdonald and his supporters.

Huntington's disclosures only complicated Allan's difficult job in Britain of raising capital for the new undertaking; British investors were already wary of Canadian railway enterprises, and the powerful Grand Trunk interests in London had seen to it that the doors of banking houses were closed to him. The breath of scandal was also scaring away friends at home – Fleming was uneasy at his association with the new railway company, and wrote to Tupper in March to enlist his help in protesting against Macdonald's apparent abdication of responsibility to Allan; Donald Smith also made a dramatic split with Macdonald in a sensational speech in the Commons. Macdonald would not soon forget Fleming's wavering and Smith's outright defection.

Macdonald's government came crashing down over the Pacific Scandal and the Liberal leader, the dour Alexander Mackenzie, was summoned to form a government in November 1873. Sir Richard Cartwright, Mackenzie's finance minister, was not an unbiased observer, but his trenchant comments accurately reflect the moral indignation of the time.

> I am neither Puritan nor Pharisee, but there are certain offences which, if proven, should banish the offender from public life for ever, and Sir John's was one of them. Consider what selling the Charter of the Canadian Pacific Railway to Sir Hugh Allan for friends to carry on an election really meant. Here was a gigantic work likely to tax the resources of Canada to the very uttermost and on the speedy and proper construction of which the whole future of Canada

might very soon come to depend, and the man who of all
others was bound by his oath of office and by every possible
consideration of honour and good faith to see that this great
work was well and properly carried out, deliberately put it
out of his own power, for a consideration, to secure that the
most ordinary safeguards should be taken to protect the
interests of the public, whose guardian and trustee he was.[1]

In the ensuing federal election, in January 1874, Mackenzie's Liberals won
a huge majority; Donald Smith returned to the Commons as one of Mackenzie's most influential supporters.

The new prime minister was a stolid Scot, of modest education, who had
come to Canada as a journeyman stone cutter and settled in Sarnia, Ontario,
where he became a successful building contractor. A prominent Liberal in the
Canadian legislature before Confederation, he later sat in both the Ontario
assembly and the federal House of Commons, serving for a year as Ontario
treasurer in the Reform government led by Edward Blake, a brilliant lawyer.
Legislation on dual representation eventually made it necessary for both
Mackenzie and Blake to leave provincial politics and opt exclusively for the
federal sphere. In opposition, they fought the Pacific railway clause of the
British Columbia terms of union, considering that it imposed an intolerable
burden on the young country's resources; once in the prime minister's office,
however, Mackenzie was pledged to find a compromise that satisfied British
Columbia, while modifying the original agreement. Blake, however, feared the
financial commitments, and he cast a long shadow over the Liberal caucus;
Mackenzie treated his former boss with deference. Proceeding with great caution, he set about to strike a new deal with British Columbia that would not
provoke a serious rupture in the Liberal Party. Blake served for a few weeks in
Mackenzie's government as minister without portfolio, but resigned in early
1874. He had been a difficult colleague and would be a thorn in Mackenzie's
flesh until he returned to cabinet as minister of justice in 1875.

Fleming pondered long where he would fit in the new order. His friendship with the Conservative Tupper was well known, but he himself had no
open political affiliations. Fleming's bigger concern was whether Mackenzie
would honour the commitment to British Columbia. Two years had passed
since the agreement with the new province, and not a mile of track had been
laid, although a good deal of survey work had been done. Mackenzie could
not have taken over at a worse time; he was saddled with the previous government's costly railway commitment, which a substantial portion of his party
opposed, and the federal treasury was in dire straits. In fact, the whole of
North America was plunging into a great depression.

Mackenzie took personal charge of the railway project, and assumed the public works portfolio for himself, setting up office in the Public Works Department in the still uncompleted West Block on Ottawa's Parliament Hill. He was taking a great deal on himself: the premiership and the public works portfolio, not to mention the demanding task of leading a party that was rent by serious factionalism. However, he had a prodigious capacity for hard work, and he was determined to prevent the sort of collusion between government and business that had undone the previous administration. The Intercolonial Board of Railway Commissioners was abolished, and control brought within the Public Works Department. Mackenzie appointed that great survivor, Brydges, as general superintendent of government railways, and insisted that all staff appointments be made on the basis of efficiency. Also at Mackenzie's insistence, Fleming gave up day-to-day involvement with the Intercolonial project early in 1874, and confined himself to the Pacific Railway.

Canada's governor general was Frederick Temple Blackwood, Earl of Dufferin; he was everything Mackenzie was not – well educated, an Ulster landlord, and full of Irish blarney. Dufferin entertained lavishly and travelled widely throughout the Dominion, always keeping himself at centre stage. Mackenzie and his followers believed that Dufferin had favoured Macdonald in the 1873 prorogation crisis, and suspected he was acting on British instructions. If Dufferin was taking orders, they would have come from the colonial secretary, Henry Howard Molyneux Herbert, Earl of Carnarvon; the two were on warm terms.

Mackenzie maintained that if the original railway conditions could not be met, British Columbia should be offered compensation. He first approached Alexander Galt to go to British Columbia to negotiate a compromise. Galt, a Conservative who had nevertheless felt compelled to oppose Macdonald over the Pacific Scandal, was a former director of the Grand Trunk, and long involved in railway affairs. When Galt declined Mackenzie's request, Casimir Gzowski was asked, but he too was unavailable. Mackenzie then turned to J.D. Edgar, the former Liberal whip who had failed re-election in 1873. Edgar went to British Columbia in February 1874 with instructions to ask the provincial government to agree to an extension of the ten-year completion deadline for the railway, in return for which the federal government would guarantee $1.5 million annually to ensure continuous construction on the mainland, and would in addition build a wagon road and telegraph line the length of the railway in the province, with the telegraph continued across the continent; the government also would immediately begin a railway line on Vancouver Island from Esquimalt to Nanaimo. (In June 1873 Macdonald, to quell agitation in Victoria, had designated Esquimalt, adjacent to Victoria, as the Pacific terminus for the railway, and the sod had been turned one day before expiry of the two-year start-up period promised in the terms of union. Macdonald's precipitate selection of a Vancouver Island terminus site stirred up a hornet's nest between the Islanders and mainlanders – another of Macdonald's legacies to Mackenzie.)

Mackenzie's proposals recalled British Columbia's own demands in 1870, but the terms of union offered by Macdonald had been far more generous; the province was not about to agree to backsliding now, so Edgar's talks with the British Columbia premier, George Walkem, were doomed to failure. Fleming's British Columbia deputy, Marcus Smith, wrote to him from Victoria on 25 May to register his concern at the situation.

> I am extremely anxious about the result of this season's sur-
> veys as the public mind here is very uneasy, and notwith-
> standing the proposals made by Mr. Edgar on behalf of the
> Dominion Government there is a very general distrust of
> the intentions of the Government to commence the actual
> construction of the railway at an early period.
>
> *We* know how impractical it would be for the
> Government to attempt to commence construction at pre-
> sent on the mainland, or even on Vancouver Island till some
> surveys are made but the public cannot or will not under-
> stand this. It is therefore extremely desirable that the surveys
> should be so far advanced this season as to enable the
> Government to determine, at least, a very considerable por-
> tion of the route of the railway on the mainland.[2]

Smith knew the realities of political horse-trading, and fully expected British Columbia and Ottawa to strike a deal soon; probably involving a commit-ment to begin construction at once on Vancouver Island, putting pressure on the survey engineers to get their work done very quickly.

The British Columbia government appealed to the imperial government in June, and the colonial secretary, Lord Carnarvon, offered to arbitrate the dispute. It was humiliating to Prime Minister Mackenzie to have the province appeal over the head of the federal government on an internal matter. In the interest of accommodation, however, he accepted Carnarvon's intervention despite hostility within his own party, and in the end Carnarvon's recommen-dations, which were submitted to Ottawa in September, did not differ sub-stantially from Mackenzie's earlier proposals.

Edward Blake, not content with Carnarvon's recommendations, wanted them approved by Parliament; Mackenzie was not keen, but eventually agreed. Blake also ensured that a special bill to provide for the Vancouver Island Railway was presented, so that the island railway would be hived off from the main line – in the event, the bill was narrowly defeated in the Senate. Blake and Mackenzie then agreed on a new railway policy, on Blake's terms. British Columbia would be offered $750,000 cash compensation in lieu of the island railway and any further delays in construction. If British Columbia did not accept, there would be no further negotiations, and no further mediation by the colonial secretary would be tolerated. Meanwhile, the federal government would proceed to build the Pacific railway as fast as physical and financial constraints permitted.

Dufferin and Carnarvon, for their part, were concerned at the threat posed to Canadian unity by the federal-provincial feud. Dufferin visited the west coast in summer 1876 to test the political waters for himself, on a mission not calculated to win Mackenzie's approval, and even less Blake's; neither man was in any mood to brook further imperial government interference. Dufferin returned to Ottawa convinced, however, that a further intervention by Carnarvon was essential, thus provoking a historic confrontation, with Mackenzie and Blake on the one side, and Dufferin on the other. Carnarvon took the path of least resistance, and implored British Columbia to be patient, since the surveys would take time; threats of separation rumbled from across the Rockies.

During the 1874 and 1875 survey seasons, Mackenzie instructed Fleming to examine the possibility of shortening the transcontinental line by incorporating it with the waterways between Lake Superior and the Red River, the so-called Dawson route of the western settlers. Fleming, however, continued to recommend a continuous line of railway. The surveys in the Lake Superior–to–Red River section were far enough advanced by early 1875 to put the two end sections under contract for grading and bridging; the first sod for the Pacific railway was turned at Fort William on 1 June and track laying began a year later, even though the surveys were far from complete. As a result, contracts were let on the basis of considerable guesswork, resulting in enormous cost over-runs, and claims by contractors against the government.

Out on the west coast Marcus Smith was all for an early start to a wagon road and telegraph line, trusting that it would keep the disgruntled mainland British Columbians quiet until the surveys were complete. It would also provide a supply route to the railway construction crews when construction eventually began.

Meanwhile, all was not well within the offices of Fleming's engineering branch in Ottawa. Mackenzie was so disturbed by the state of Pacific railway accounts when he took office that he ordered all vouchers to be brought to him. Shortly thereafter a huge trunk, two metres long and a metre wide, stuffed full of vouchers, was deposited on his floor. It was more than even Mackenzie's sharp pencil could cope with. Fleming had been a reluctant accountant from the outset, and had asked the previous government to relieve him of this duty, but it was only now that Mackenzie discovered the extent of the problem. He brought in an accountant in November 1874 to sort things out.

A parliamentary public accounts committee inquiry into the financial disbursement and accounting procedures of the survey branch opened in April 1875. Fleming told the committee:

> I felt that the direction of engineering matters was quite enough for me personally to attend to, that I might fairly leave, and in fact I was compelled to leave wholly to others, the duty of attending to purchases and disbursements and keeping an account of the expenditure incurred thereby ... When two seasons had passed I found that serious difficulties in connection with the commissariat branch of the service had arisen, involving me personally in a great deal of trouble which I really ought to have been spared. I therefore applied to the Minister of Public Works to be entirely relieved of even nominal responsibility in the matter of accounts.[3]

Fleming, with no fondness for bookkeeping procedures, had operated without giving any real day-to-day direction. He had appointed William Wallace commissariat officer, paymaster, and accountant of the eastern division of the survey in May 1871. Sums of money were deposited in Fleming's bank account to be disbursed by him for the survey, and he had delegated responsibility to his staff with an insouciance that the committee of inquiry found quite incredible. Fleming had simply let Wallace get on with it, taking no security from him for the public funds entrusted to him, and expecting him to keep a correct account of all expenditures. Wallace held the position until he resigned to run for Parliament in July 1872, but money continued to be deposited to the "Wallace account" after his formal resignation. More than half a million dollars was disbursed on the eastern division from May 1871 to June 1873, the period covered by the Wallace account, but there were no vouchers to account for a sizeable portion. The parliamentary inquiry, not surprisingly, found that the system of paying large sums of public money to the credit of private individuals was unprofessional and improper. There had been no check on prices paid by Wallace; he had no instructions concerning where or from whom supplies should be purchased. Fleming pleaded the problems of coping with new and uncertain areas in a major new enterprise.

He was critical of Wallace for not delegating sufficient authority, yet when Wallace left Fleming assumed the responsibilities himself, becoming paymaster and scrapping the commissariat system, and thereby adding to his burdens in an area in which he had no expertise.

Mackenzie was horrified at Fleming's slipshod oversight of public funds, and testified before the parliamentary inquiry:

> The fact that Mr. Fleming stated to me that he was not aware of any of the payments made to Mr. Wallace (following Wallace's resignation) until he went to the bank and got a statement, showed how loose and improper the system was … I attribute a very large portion of the irregularity to the fact that Mr. Fleming had undertaken and was discharging duties totally incompatible with the responsibility devolving upon him, duties which he should never have been burdened with, and ought never to have assumed.[4]

The storm over the Wallace account only came to public notice in December 1874 when Thomas Steers Jr., a spiteful junior clerk in the survey branch, gave an inaccurate but still damaging statement to the *Ottawa Citizen*. Steers was arrested at the beginning of December for allegedly absconding with railway funds received on the sale of surplus survey stores; he was charged but not convicted when he claimed his right to payment for extra services performed during his time in the survey branch. It was just one more proof of the disorder in the branch under Fleming's control. Mackenzie instituted sweeping changes to bring the accounting procedures into line.

> The whole system of managing the accounts of the Pacific Railway Survey may be characterised in two words – as being most unbusinesslike; and it was of such a nature as to make it absolutely impossible to ensure accuracy or correctness, and left to the temptation to every one to do wrong. I have taken the necessary measures to have all that corrected, and now no money is paid out except through the regular accountant, Mr. Radford, and the engineers are thereby relieved from all responsibility, which they never should have had and never should have assumed, and the Department might supervise those matters, and thereby make the survey a branch of the Public Works Department so far as the regular authorising of payments and making payments were concerned.[5]

Fleming was dogged by a multitude of problems; it was he who had to reconcile the government's half-hearted commitment to the railway project with the necessity of being seen to lay track in British Columbia's direction. Money was scarce and political patronage rampant; the politicians continued to encumber Fleming with staff who were ill trained to perform their assigned duties and sometimes even ill disposed to defer to the professional judgement of the chief engineer. Fleming, and later Mackenzie's government, was plagued by insubordination and deviousness within the engineering department; the worst offenders were Charles Horetzky the survey photographer and Marcus Smith.

Nobody could get along with Charles Horetzky; he was arrogant, self-serving and truculent. Horetzky was directly responsible to Marcus Smith, who was in charge of the British Columbia operations, but Smith had no control over him. Whenever anyone tried to put Horetzky in his place he threatened to call on the higher authority of his political friends in Ottawa, and *tell all* (without ever saying what there was to tell) about Smith. If he was not treated with kid gloves, Horetzky was not above going direct to Mackenzie with his grievances.

The worst of the political patronage showed itself in 1877 when Mackenzie went on an economy drive and ordered wholesale cuts in the engineering staff. Smith was expected to wield the axe in Fleming's absence, but in a manner to ensure that only certain heads rolled; Smith wrote to Fleming about the invidious position he found himself in.

> The inconsistency of this economical fit is shown by the appointment of new men in the very places where I had instructions to reduce the staff – young men forced on the Government by the importunity of their political friends – consequently, the staff is being deteriorated without the expenses being much reduced. And at the same time the staff of Purveyors especially at Prince Arthur District and British Columbia is excessively large, costly and inefficient. I don't think I exceed fact by stating that both the cost of surveys and engineering on construction is 25 per cent more than it was under the sole management of the engineers.[6]

No one, however, was more adept than Smith himself in pulling political strings.

CHAPTER 8

BATTLE OF THE ROUTES

The surveys of the Pacific region were proving difficult, and disagreement among Fleming's engineering staff over the most suitable route through the Rockies and to the Pacific coast opened another deep fissure in the engineering branch. Initially, there was something like a consensus in favour of a route through the Rockies at the Yellowhead Pass, and then to Bute Inlet and across the Strait by steamer to Vancouver Island. This plan obviously was favoured by Victoria interests. Fleming, for his part, was satisfied from what he witnessed himself in 1872 that the Yellowhead was the best way through the Rockies, but he favoured a more southerly route from there along the Thompson and Fraser rivers to a terminus at Burrard Inlet on the mainland. It was shorter, and avoided the costly steamer crossing to Vancouver Island. While the mainlanders were all for Fleming's route, the Vancouver Island interests were, naturally, not quite so enthusiastic; it became a battle royal between the two.

As far as Fleming was concerned it was a question of engineering pure and simple; no fewer than ten routes from the Yellowhead to various points up and down the Pacific coast had been surveyed. Other passes through the Rockies were examined but none was proved to Fleming's satisfaction to be better than the Yellowhead. Some of his principal assistants, however, had other ideas; Moberly, for example, was passionately committed to Howse Pass, south of the Yellowhead. Horetzky was equally convinced that the line should run in a more northerly direction via the Peace River country through Pine Pass to Port Simpson on the Pacific coast. But the sharpest thorn in Fleming's side was Marcus Smith – Smith had worked for Fleming since the early days of the Intercolonial, and was now in charge of the Pacific railway's western region. Although he got on well enough with Fleming at the outset, from 1877 on he was unrelenting in his challenge to Fleming's authority as he canvassed for the alternative Pine Pass–Bute Inlet route. Fleming, meanwhile, knew the pressures the government was under to have done with the surveys as fast as possible, and get on with construction.

Fleming was criticized for making virtually no personal inspections of western operations after his Pacific trek in 1872; however, since 1873, he had been unable to walk for more than a short distance at a time after seriously spraining his ankle. He had contemplated surveying Bute Inlet and Gardiner Inlet for himself in 1875, but the nagging ankle pain discouraged him. Fleming wrote to Mackenzie in July 1875 about his generally indifferent health, and said that once the Intercolonial was finished he would need an extended break. By the beginning of 1876 Fleming was on the point of exhaustion. His condition was aggravated by domestic problems – his youngest brother, John, had never recovered his health damaged on the prairie expedition with Hind years before, and died in 1876; Jeanie was extremely ill and indeed came close to death, tended by the family physician, Charles Tupper. Mackenzie gave Fleming a year's leave of absence, and he took the family to England for a complete change of scenery and an undisturbed rest. Fleming's critics, however, never rested; Nova Scotia politician A.G. Jones wrote to Mackenzie in May 1877:

> The papers here are discussing Fleming's leaving for England and I enclose you an item from today's *Herald.* I thought it queer his going away just now and before I saw any public reference to it I thought he was leaving to get out of the way. I don't trust him a bit. He is too intimate with Tupper and all his gang and you may depend you will have to keep your eyes open and watch him closely. He and Tupper were concerned with the Pictou road and will always pull together.[1]

Others in the Liberal Party were concerned that the engineering department harboured a Conservative nest of vipers. Oliver Mowat wrote to Mackenzie in July:

> I have a letter from Prince Arthurs Landing in which it is mentioned that every engineer and employee of the Pacific Railway almost to a man are warm sympathisers with the enemy. In another part of the letter Mr. Frank Moberly's name is mentioned. I do not know whether he is employed on the road but he is mentioned as President and originator of the Conservative Association of Thunder Bay and has been attacking Mr. Dawson who is supporting the Government here … It seems also that a party of Conservatives here planned a trip in that quarter to possess themselves of information out of which to attack your Government, the party consisting of Senator Macpherson and Smith, Mr. Kirkpatrick and others.[2]

Mackenzie's agreement to let Fleming go to England had not been without condition; he instructed Fleming to talk to various English contractors and financiers, with a view to interesting them in constructing the Pacific railway under contract. The terms offered would include the grant of 8,100 hectares and $10,000 per mile, and Fleming solicited tenders on those terms for some months. No one was interested; not a single offer was made. It is scarcely surprising: the Intercolonial, after all, had cost three times as much per mile to construct. How could any contractor conceivably be attracted by such a losing proposition? If the railway was going to be built, the government would have to manage the work itself, with contracts let on a schedule system and contractors paid for work as actually performed. Circumstances were forcing them to adopt the very method Fleming had fought for in vain on the Intercolonial.

With Fleming absent, things quickly spun out of control in the engineering department; Mackenzie summoned him back at the beginning of 1877 to put things right. By this time his reputation spanned the Atlantic and he had been made a Commander of the Order of St. Michael and St. George (CMG) – to Mackenzie's great annoyance, since he had not been consulted. Back in Canada Fleming was called before the Commons committee on public accounts to give evidence on the Georgian Bay branch of the Pacific railway. Two branches of the main line were proposed – Winnipeg to Pembina, and Georgian Bay. It was the responsibility of the contractors to conduct surveys on the branch lines; the contractor for the Georgian Bay line, Mr. Foster, was unable to fulfil his contract. At the time, Foster was also in difficulty with the Canada Central Railway. It had been discovered that Foster had appropriated rails purchased for the Georgian Bay line and diverted them to the Canada Central. Nearly two thousand tons of rails were purchased for the Georgian Bay branch but not used, and the price of rails dropped after the order was delivered. Fleming was in England when Foster helped himself to the Georgian Bay rails for his work on the Canada Central. The affair accentuated the lack of control over the engineering department.

In the course of his parliamentary testimony, Fleming made clear his view that the building of the transcontinental line would take a great deal longer than was generally imagined.

> *Mackenzie:* I asked you the other day if you were of the opinion the Pacific Railway could be built in ten years, and you said it could not; what time do you suppose it would take to build that railway?

Fleming:	I should think nearly double that time would be spent on it.
Tupper:	Do I understand you to say the road could not be built in ten years, or to build it in ten years would make the cost so excessive that no one would be justified in pushing it so far?
Fleming:	I mean to say it ought not to be built in ten years.
Tupper:	I want you to say whether the road could be built in ten years if you had the money to do it.
Fleming:	We do not use the word impossible in any undertaking if you give us money enough.[3]

With Fleming away during most of this period, Marcus Smith was in charge of the engineering department; he moved to Ottawa to oversee the operations, and put Henry Cambie in charge of the British Columbia division. Smith was more and more certain that a northern route through the Rockies and across British Columbia was the better course – he had heard reports of rich soil in the north, a northern line would be closer to the gold fields, and a northern terminus would be ideally suited for trade with China and Japan. Smith was strategically placed, with Fleming out of the way, to promote the Pine Pass–Bute Inlet route, and he lobbied politicians relentlessly; he pushed so hard that he succeeded in antagonizing not only his staff but also the prime minister.

Mackenzie wanted Fleming back in Ottawa; someone had to sit on Smith. In his 1877 annual Pacific Railway report to the government, Fleming acknowledged there were conflicting views on the best western terminus, and proposed that the opinion of the Admiralty, long familiar with the Pacific coastline, be sought; in due course this was done and the navy reported in favour of Burrard Inlet. However, the 1877 survey season had finally convinced the determined Marcus Smith that he was right; in May he instructed one of his engineering staff, Joseph Hunter, to make a preliminary survey of the more northerly route. Meanwhile, Smith's British Columbia deputy, Henry Cambie, found himself unwittingly caught in the middle – he knew that the prime minister leaned toward Fleming's recommended Fraser River–Burrard Inlet route, but his immediate supervisor, Marcus Smith, was intent on the northern route to Bute Inlet. Mackenzie did not trust Smith and deliberately bypassed him to deal directly with Cambie. Cambie, for his part, was an engineer pure and simple, and he was acutely embarrassed by the difficult position he had been put in. In despair, he turned to the chief he had served since 1863. He wrote to Fleming:

> A couple of days ago Mr. Mackenzie sent for me and dis-
> cussed the Fraser River Route for upwards of an hour, and
> then asked me to embody our conversation in a letter to him,
> which he wants to forward to Lord Carnarvon. He by asking
> me direct questions elicited opinions from me on subjects
> which I should never have thought of referring to had he not
> done so. For instance he asked me what I thought of the
> grades on Bute Inlet route, as compared with the Fraser, and
> the power of a locomotive on each. And if I thought it possi-
> ble to have a ferry from Burrard Inlet to some point on
> Vancouver Island – suggesting head of Saanich Inlet and to
> have a Railway from that place to Esquimault, for use in case
> of hostilities with the US now that San Juan is in their hands.
> These are most embarrassing questions for me, and will bring
> me into direct conflict with Mr. Smith and should never
> have been asked of me. I can hardly refuse the Premier how-
> ever – and have taken Smellie as my adviser, who will assist
> me to write as noncommittal a letter as possible. He offered
> to keep the matter private if I wished but I declined and
> requested him to tell Mr. Smith and told him that I shall
> hand a copy of whatever letter I write to Mr. Smith.[4]

Smellie, the *chef de cabinet* in the engineering office, helped Cambie compose
a correct but cautious letter, which avoided giving Prime Minister Mackenzie
exactly what he wanted, namely, a letter clearly setting out all the advantages
of the Fraser River route, and the disadvantages of the Pine Pass–Bute Inlet
route. However, their effort was in vain. Mackenzie was not satisfied; he gave
Cambie a few more days to come up with something more along the lines of
what he wanted.

Extravagant spending by the commissariat officers in British Columbia
drew Cambie reluctantly into yet another conflict with Smith. One of the
principal commissariat officers in British Columbia, Mr. Robson, was fingered by Smith for mismanagement of funds; a charge later found to be
largely baseless. When Smith subsequently was called to account for the false
accusation, he put the blame on Cambie's shoulders, although the unfortu-
nate Cambie was entirely innocent.

Smith had managed until now not to cause serious offence to Fleming;
perhaps because Fleming was, for the moment, so far removed from the
scene. Indeed, Smith still imagined that he could bring Fleming around to
acknowledging the superior qualities of the northern route ahead of the
Yellowhead–Fraser River. Smith made an extensive survey of the Pine River

country and returned overwhelmed by the fertility of the soil; he wrote to Fleming about his findings:

> We still know too little about it to make a fair comparison with other routes – but it would appear not to be longer than that by the Yellowhead Pass and the work generally lighter – but what appears to me of more importance that either cost or length is that it reduces the length of barren lands by several hundred miles.[5]

It seemed to Marcus Smith, however, that the federal government was hell-bent on the Yellowhead–to–Burrard Inlet route, and that desperate measures were called for. He spread a story that Mackenzie and other important public figures had a personal stake in Burrard Inlet. Smith wrote to Fleming with his allegation:

> At Victoria I found out about this Burrard Inlet mania which is a huge land job in which the Minister and his friends are concerned. The latter certainly are from the Lieutenant Governor downwards. It was first started by Lord Dufferin in 1876 while you were in England and I was away north of Lake Superior. His Excellency was much annoyed at not succeeding in gaining the leading men of Vancouver over to his views that is to abandon the Railway and leave its carrying out to the good faith of the Canadian Government, or as they expressed it to take 10 cents on the dollar. He even had solicited assistance on private grounds saying that it would help him so much in his diplomatic career if he could succeed in bringing the Dominion and Provincial Government to a mutual understanding – but they were inflexible and his lordship was very angry and revenged himself by seizing on rumours against myself in connection with the Fraser route and actually promising the people of the Fraser Valley – as they allege – that we would endeavour to get the line by that route. The first I heard of it was on my return home last year when Smellie told me that by instructions of the Minister he telegraphed Richards the Lieutenant Governor to instruct Cambie to commence the survey of the Fraser. This was done at the wishes of the Governor General ... I think I know how to defend myself; Of course I know that the Minister can and will dismiss me

and he is trying to do so at a month's notice – but I am determined to *die hard* and shall expose his tricks – the whole thing is a trick to get votes and enrich his friends. I have it on good authority that the Government has no intention of building the west end of the line at all but only making a demonstration.[6]

Smith was digging in his heels, and imagined he could get away with it if only he could bring his chief in on his side, but he badly misjudged Fleming's commitment to the Yellowhead Pass route. Hopeful that the forthcoming federal election would bring a change of government, Smith made a bid for time, and recommended that a further look be taken into alternative routes. His report to the government of the 1877 survey was patently tilted in favour of the Pine Pass–Bute Inlet option, emphasizing the vast expanse of fertile land in the north, and by contrast the barren land west of the Yellowhead. Mackenzie was at his wits' end; unless a route was settled quickly the impending federal election would overtake the government, with who could say what electoral consequences in British Columbia?

Working relations within the engineering department were reduced to a shambles as Mackenzie played Cambie off against Smith, and Smith rode roughshod over anyone who got in his way. Fleming, back in England again, watched from afar as matters came to the boiling point, through the regular letters from his loyal office staff back in Ottawa, W.B. Smellie and Tom Burpe. Smellie reported to Fleming that Mackenzie was determined to get rid of Smith after learning that he was playing into the hands of the opposition.

Once again, in 1878, Mackenzie telegraphed to Fleming to return to Ottawa immediately; Fleming stood before the prime minister in his West Block office. As Fleming recorded the meeting,

> "Sandford," the Prime Minister said, "I have lost confidence in Marcus Smith; I haven't spoken to him on any subject for a couple of months. I believe that Smith is strongly biased. So, I want you, Sandford, to take up the whole subject, and give your opinion. If you endorse Smith's views let me know; if you do not, report accordingly; but before being guided by Smith's report, I want to have the benefit of your opinion.
>
> "And Sandford, you must consider Marcus Smith as no longer an officer of the Department. He hasn't received his dismissal yet, but he is as good as dismissed, and you are not at liberty, therefore, to consult him any longer."[7]

Upon leaving Mackenzie's office, Fleming went straight to his own and sent for Smith. He repeated to his deputy, word for word, the prime minister's instructions, and explained to Smith that he was obliged to use his own judgement, and would no longer be consulting him.

Fleming then closeted himself with all the available and often conflicting documents – Smith's survey report, Cambie's report, and several from the field crews; within days he had produced the recommendation Mackenzie was looking for and, as before, he favoured Burrard Inlet. As a sop to Smith, and with a residual uncertainty that must have been galling to Mackenzie, Fleming did recommend that more surveys be undertaken in northern British Columbia, just in case it could be shown that there was a less costly route through the province than the Thompson and Fraser River line. Fleming faithfully incorporated Smith's contrary findings in his report, but purposely dropped Smith's map, which he considered misleading in the categorical way it represented the extent of fertile land in the north. Smith was, of course, furious.

With the report on Mackenzie's desk, and the battle of the routes, as he hoped, won, Fleming returned to England yet again. Mackenzie had his eye on the calendar – it was election year, and the voters of British Columbia were unhappy with the state of progress on the railway line. Fleming was instructed when he arrived back in England to place the following advertisement in all the railway and financial papers, and in the leading commercial papers of London, Liverpool, Edinburgh, Glasgow, and Dublin:

> Canadian Pacific Railway
> To Capitalists and Contractors
> The Government of Canada will receive proposals for construction and working a line of Railway extending from the Province of Ontario to the waters of the Pacific Ocean, the distance being about 2000 miles. Memorandums of information for parties proposing to Tender will be forwarded on application as underneath. Engineers' Reports, maps of the country to be traversed, profiles of the surveyed line, specifications of preliminary works, copies of the Act of the Parliament of Canada under which it is proposed the Railway is to be constructed, descriptions of the natural features of the country and its agricultural and mineral resources, and other information, may be seen on application at this Department, or to the Engineer-in-Chief at the Canadian Government Offices, 31 Queen Victoria St., E.C., London.

Sealed Tenders, marked, "Tenders for Pacific Railway," will be received, addressed to the undersigned, until the 1st day of December next.

Ottawa, May 20, 1878
F. Braun, Secretary,
Public Works Department, Ottawa

The deadline for receipt of tenders was later extended to 1 January 1879. The government settled on the Fraser River–Burrard Inlet route in July 1878, two months before the federal election. Mackenzie's design fell apart, however, as the election results came in; after 17 September the Liberals were out of office in a devastating election defeat, and Macdonald's Conservatives were securely back at the helm.

CHAPTER 9

DERAILED

No one could have been more delighted with the election outcome than Marcus Smith, who saw in it a heaven-sent renewed chance to keep his Pine Pass–Bute Inlet line alive. Smith had conspired to bring about the defeat of the Mackenzie government; John Robson, a British Columbia Liberal, wrote to Mackenzie in September 1879 to explain Smith's part in the party's heavy losses on the west coast.

> And to these efforts must be added the influence of Marcus Smith, who, in passing through the District in the fall of 1877, everywhere and most industriously spoke of your railway policy as shuffling humbug, declaring that you had really not the slightest intention of going on with the work in British Columbia and predicting very positively the return to power of the Conservatives, the only men, he said, from whom Columbia could hope for a railway – statements which, coming from such a source were *bound* to have considerable influence.[1]

Smith must have cheered aloud when Macdonald, having gone down to personal defeat in Kingston, decided to represent Victoria in the Commons. The only fly in the ointment for Smith was Macdonald's appointment of Fleming's old friend Charles Tupper as minister of railways. Still fuming at Fleming's exclusion of his map from the 1878 survey report, Smith no longer had a good word to say about him; he wrote caustically to Fleming implying that he had acted out of self-interest in advancing the Yellowhead–Burrard Inlet route. In fact, the idea is implausible – Fleming would not have vacillated so long if he had had a vested interest; on the other hand, Smith's residence and associations in British Columbia had largely centred on Victoria and Vancouver Island, and it has been suggested that he had himself bought speculative land in the Bute Inlet area.

The artful Mr. Smith meant to force Fleming out if he could, but without appearing to threaten the powerful Tupper, who was generally considered

Macdonald's heir apparent. Smith's tack was to try to convince the Tories that the chief engineer had acted rather too narrowly in the former Liberal government's interest in recommending Burrard Inlet. If Tupper continued to support the Liberals' – and Fleming's – choice of Burrard Inlet, in opposition to his party's longstanding support for Bute Inlet, his leadership aspirations might suffer a fatal blow.

Smith was unrelenting in his attack, bombarding Tupper and other ministers with letters accusing Fleming; so much so that Fleming was driven to write to the public works minister in May 1879 to set the record straight. Fleming reiterated that there was not a single shred of evidence to support Smith's contention that a hundred million acres of potential farmland lay north of the Fraser River route. But Smith's campaign of vilification was beginning to bite; the press and public were taking notice, and Conservatives were asking questions. The chairman of the Senate's public accounts committee, Senator David Macpherson, opened a public investigation in March 1879 into Pacific Railway affairs; Macpherson was friendly with Macdonald, but no friend of either Tupper or Fleming. Smith's Victoria friends kept up the heat in the Commons; the Victoria member, Amor de Cosmos, tried in March to get Tupper to release Smith's suppressed map, but Tupper steadfastly refused. He told the House that explorations carried out during the past season had satisfied him that Marcus Smith's map was misleading. In fact, by now virtually all members, except those from Vancouver Island, accepted the Burrard Inlet site.

Prepared as he was thus far to stick by Fleming, it was clear to Tupper that political pressure was mounting, both in the Commons and in the Senate, with Macpherson's committee probing deeper into the operations of the engineering office. In May 1879 Tupper ordered new surveys in the area favoured by Marcus Smith, but there was little comfort for Smith – they would be conducted, under Fleming's general direction, by his faithful deputy, Henry Cambie. Smith's plan to alienate Tupper from Fleming needed more work.

Macdonald and Tupper were determined to get the Pacific Railway project moving. The time was propitious; the Intercolonial was complete and in successful operation, and North America was pulling itself out of the great depression that had haunted Mackenzie's years in office. The Pacific Railway Act was subjected to radical surgery once more in May 1879, with the project put on a whole new footing – 40.4 million hectares of land were reserved for sale, with the express purpose of funding the railway, and a board of commissioners had been constituted to oversee the arrangement. Railway construction and colonization went hand in hand for the Tories; if the railway was to become a viable proposition, more people would have to be attracted to settle in Canada.

Immigrants had already been attracted to southern Manitoba; John Macoun, the botanist, reported to the new government that the southern plains were far and away more bountiful than the more northerly region, so much of which was muskeg swamp. Tupper accordingly changed the policy of the Liberals, and scrapped the route from Selkirk north to the narrows of Lake Manitoba, in favour of bringing it south of the Lake, despite Fleming's contrary advice – the southerly route added forty-eight kilometres to the line and encountered more difficult grades and sharp curves.

Tupper announced in May that 200 kilometres of railway line would be built in British Columbia; he let a contract in August for 100 kilometres west of Winnipeg, and advertised tenders for another 160. The line would run south of Lake Manitoba to Portage la Prairie and Brandon. The town of Winnipeg offered, if given a branch line, to find the means of bridging the river there at its own expense; the deal was irresistible to Tupper, who saw in it the chance to save close to $500,000, even though it meant an extra 25.6 kilometres of track.

It was well known that Tupper favoured putting the whole of the Pacific Railway under private contract. It was known further that Tupper's friend Sandford Fleming was close to Donald A. Smith and his cousin George Stephen, president of the Bank of Montreal, who were likely prime contenders for the Pacific Railway contract. Fleming had been invited in May 1879 to join Smith, Stephen, and others in buying up the St. Paul, Minneapolis, and Manitoba Railway. They tried to interest Fleming in becoming a partner in the venture, but he declined, preferring not to run the risk of appearing to be in conflict of interest with his duties as the government's chief engineer on the Pacific Railway. Smith, it will be recalled, fell out with Macdonald over the Pacific Scandal. Prominent Conservatives, however, were associated with another syndicate that had its eye on the mammoth railway deal. Sir Hugh Allan had regrouped his Montreal-based Merchant's Bank group in 1877; among its executive directors were James Ferrer of the Grand Trunk and John McLennan, both Conservative members of Parliament. C.J. Brydges was a vice-president of the bank. Senator David Macpherson was politically allied with this group, which distrusted Tupper and Fleming.

Tupper's position as Macdonald's heir apparent was not entirely secure; it was suggested, for example, that Dalton McCarthy, a personal friend of Macdonald's, aspired to succeed Macdonald as prime minister and might do so. J.W. Longley writes, in his life of Tupper:

> It is certain that a cabal was active within the secret councils
> of the party in pressing for the removal of Mr. Fleming from

his post as Chief Engineer. What transpired in those private discussions in the caucus cannot be related, but is is known that dislike and suspicion of the energetic Minister of Railways was to some extent the occasion of this move on the part of Conservative members to have a house-cleaning in connection with Railway construction.[2]

The chief strength of the cabal was among Ontario members, and Tupper's defence was weakened by his past and continuing association with Fleming.

The government confirmed the Fraser River–Burrard Inlet route on 4 October, and tenders were called for mid-November; the route battle was over, and Marcus Smith had lost. He gave full vent to his anger, lashing out at Fleming's engineering competence and the Fleming-Tupper combination with a battery of letters to anti-Tupper factions in the Conservative Party. He knew exactly who in the party did not like Tupper: Charles Brydges, for example, who had been peremptorily dropped by Tupper as general superintendent of government railways. Smith wrote to Brydges and Senator Macpherson in an all-out effort to sow suspicion about Fleming; they, in turn, reported his allegations to Macdonald. Macpherson wrote to the prime minister:

> It is universally said that Fleming's administration is as bad as ever and that his chief sees with *his* eyes and hears with *his* ears all boding the reverse of good to the Government.[3]

And, concerning the location of the line in Manitoba:

> It is openly said that the reason for trying to force a crossing of the river as near to Selkirk as possible is to promote the interest of a band of land speculators numbering among them some of the Engineers. To this last fact (I have *reason* to believe *it is* a fact) is ascribed in the West this Northern location so culpably recommended by Fleming and adopted by Mackenzie.[4]

Then Macpherson buried the knife deep.

> It is not strengthening to hear the Minister and Chief Engineer spoke of as Siamese Twins and that it is futile to contemplate a change of Engineer although disastrous mismanagement is rampant.[5]

Apart from Brydges, Alexander Galt, who also was associated with the GTR construction and a Conservative, would have liked to have Fleming's job; he told Macdonald that, with Fleming, the construction of the railway would be neither speedy nor economical. Galt claimed that for his part he could save millions of dollars and months of time; he added that Fleming seemed incapable of grasping what the country wanted and what it could do with its resources.

Macdonald could see the damage Tupper's association with Fleming was doing to the party; the prime minister owed a great deal to Tupper, who had been his most fervent supporter during the difficult days of the 1873 crisis, but he owed nothing to Fleming. In November, Macdonald summoned Tupper, and put it to him straight: Fleming had to be contained before he became an unbearable liability for the party. Tupper, in turn, immediately put pressure on Fleming to force his staff into greater efficiency, threatening him with dismissal if he failed to put the government's need for economy and haste first. The old friendship, which had weathered so many battles, was under tremendous strain, and Tupper was torn between personal and party loyalty.

Meanwhile, Smith never let up his attack on Tupper and Fleming; he wrote to a British Columbia friend in January 1880:

> Besides the motive he had for the sake of consistency to abide by the Burrard Inlet route he (Fleming) is consumed with an unquenchable jealousy of myself and others of the staff who have shown any independence and will oppose with all his power anything proposed by me. Unfortunately he has unbounded control over the Minister of Public Works. The voice of scandal assigns a cause for this influence. It appears that years ago when Tupper was Premier of Nova Scotia Parliament Fleming was appointed Engineer to carry out some Railway work. He soon broke down the contractors and got the work into his own hands and got a young man appointed (nominally) Engineer in his place. He made a large fortune and it is said Tupper shared it – he certainly at least winked at it and the pair have been inseparable ever since … Fleming has fallen very low in public opinion and has only one or two supporters in the Government. It is thought they will find it difficult to carry him over the session. I am still a power but the bête noire of the Government – for I not only persist in sticking to the truth but *insist* in having the *whole* truth laid before the public –

and if they persist in suppressing my Reports and maps I will publish them on my own account.[6]

Smith was pushing to have the Yale–Kamloops, British Columbia, section – which had already been put out to contract by Tupper – reduced to a local line to allow more time to develop and explore the northern route. He was not above fanning the flames of current scandal, hoping to increase Tupper's embarrassment.

> There are ugly rumours about these contracts. An American firm with whom Oppenheimer is connected put in a tender two million dollars higher than those to whom the contracts are awarded and this same firm has since bought these contracts giving a considerable bonus to the parties who held them – The scandal is that Tupper and Fleming are the real contractors. I however don't think that this is the correct version though no doubt there will be certain provisos attached to the contracts which it is said will be signed immediately.[7]

Senator Macpherson sent a memorandum to the prime minister at the beginning of February concerning the management of CPR affairs, finding fault with Fleming's performance. Macpherson charged that Fleming's long absence in England showed neglect of or indifference to duty. Tupper called Fleming into his West Block office and showed him Macpherson's note. It was getting harder to stand by his friend.

The storm against Fleming struck in Parliament with full fury on 3 March when the member for Glengarry, John McLennan, rose in the House to move that all contracts let on the CPR up to the end of the previous year, together with the original estimates of costs and the actual costs so far incurred, be tabled for review. Thus began a rancorous debate, which mauled Fleming's reputation and hastened his downfall. McLennan could not find words sufficient to express his outrage at Fleming and his district engineer in Manitoba, James Rowan; he blamed them for the enormous cost over-runs on construction between Lake Superior and the Red River. For example, McLennan charged, on section 15 between Cross Lake and Rat Portage, a distance of fifty-nine kilometres, costs were forty percent over estimate because of changes in the character of the work after the contract had been let. He accused Fleming of dereliction of duty for failing to be on hand to supervise affairs and ensure that the government's wishes were carried out faithfully by the engineering department. McLennan questioned the peculiar arrangement that seemed to exist between the former Liberal government and its chief engineer. McLennan concluded that Fleming was out of control or, "the only other position that could be assumed is that he occupied the position which an architect occupies who leads one on." The prime minister interjected, "Led on by a towering ambition." The abandonment of Fleming was all but complete.

Tupper took the floor to rebut, though in conciliatory tones, the charges against Fleming. He explained why Fleming had worked for so many years on the CPR at no fixed salary. When Fleming was first appointed to the Pacific Railway his Intercolonial salary was only two hundred dollars less than that of a minister. It was considered inappropriate that the chief engineer's salary should be more. Shortly after that Fleming's salary had ceased. With the completion of the Intercolonial his health broke down and he left for England; the salary question had been deferred until his return.

The former prime minister, Alexander Mackenzie, explained to the House why he had trusted Fleming so much.

> I did not feel myself capable of gauging the capacity of Mr. Fleming as a civil engineer; he was possessed of the qualities of an author as well as those of an engineer, and there was a great deal of importance to be attached to the ability, which as an author he possessed, in preparing and presenting reports, so as to make his views sufficiently known to the Government and the public. Looking back on my five years' term of office, I would be prepared at this moment to endorse nearly all that was done under Mr. Fleming's direction, making allowance for difficulties which could not be foreseen.[8]

Another member of Parliament, Simon J. Dawson, introduced a whole litany of further complaints against Fleming, Rowan, and Mackenzie. He suggested that Fleming wielded too much power over the government, and proposed that a board of engineers be set up to advise on practical matters. He also condemned Fleming's authoritarian rule within the engineering department, specifically mentioning the suppression of Marcus Smith's map. According to Dawson there had been incredible mismanagement and ineptitude in the conduct of surveys, causing enormous delays and cost overruns.

Time was running out for Fleming. On 26 March he handed Tupper a long memorandum spelling out in great detail his reply to the damaging allegations against him in Parliament and the press. Fleming recorded that as he handed the note to Tupper he "did not conceal from me ... that there was an outside clamour into which political feelings entered, which was embarrassing to the Government."[9]

A month later Tupper's supply bill was before the House, requesting the necessary funds for railway construction. This offered yet another occasion for the governing Conservatives to score political points against Mackenzie and the former Liberal government's ill-fated railway policy. The opposition was caught in a cleft stick – it was obliged to be critical of the government's "extravagant" estimates, but in so doing it exposed itself to charges that the cost escalations arose from miscalculations when it formed the government. Tupper castigated Mackenzie for letting contracts without adequate surveys, particularly in two sections – east from Red River for 182.4 kilometres, and 180.8 kilometres running west from Lake Superior. He heaped abuse on Mackenzie for his half-hearted commitment to the terms of union with British Columbia, even in the watered-down version of the Carnarvon compromise.

Mackenzie disclaimed responsibility for the surveys and insinuated that Fleming might have given him misleading advice.

> I received the approximate quantities from Mr. Fleming in good faith, after the country had been visited by himself after the surveyors had been over it, and if Mr. Fleming led me astray in giving false quantities, there is no epithet too strong to address him. But until Mr. Fleming says that, with his own lips, I will not believe that he could be guilty of such an act of perfidy. Having Mr. Fleming's estimates of the approximate quantities I proceeded to let the works.[10]

Tupper had Mackenzie on the run; he pressed the attack against the former prime minister, while trying to save Fleming's skin. Tupper asserted that Fleming had made clear from the outset that his estimates for the line from Fort William to Selkirk were based only on "guesswork." The beleaguered opposition leader once again deflected the attack to Fleming.

> If Mr. Fleming, or any other engineer, now says that he had no intention of setting forth those specific quantities as approximately accurate, I can only say that Department was grossly deceived, and the Minister was grossly deceived.[11]

Fleming had all but run out of friends on both sides of the House.

There were plenty of other signs of trouble for Fleming at the beginning of 1880. The Montreal *Gazette*, and its editor, the Conservative member of Parliament Thomas White, joined the campaign to dump Fleming by printing an anonymous letter, signed only "Thistle." Thistle betrayed a detailed working knowledge of the railway works in Manitoba, and wrote at great length about inadequate surveys and badly miscalculated estimates. The mystery letter-writer claimed that costly mistakes had been made by the engineering staff through human ignorance and folly, and he delivered a vicious broadside against Fleming:

> In no civilized country has there been an attempt to impose upon the people as has been done here, and none other than the Canadians would submit for a single day to such an imposition. The whole of the engineering done on the line has been nothing but a continual series of the grossest blunders, resulting from thorough incompetence, and can only be characterized as a huge engineering fraud, and the sooner that Canada is rid of this incubus the better for her prosperity, as the ignorance is not only imposing an enormous cost on our people but is likewise solely accountable for the altogether inexcusable delay in completing the several sections of the road now under contract. In view of the gross bungling it behoves every lover of Canada and everyone interested in her prosperity to do their utmost to forward the general interest, and I have in this communication endeavoured to do mine.[12]

The *Gazette* had disagreed with Fleming's methods of operation since the beginning of the Intercolonial project, particularly with regard to the contracts issue. On 7 January, following up on the Thistle letter, the *Gazette* continued the attack on Mackenzie and Fleming's practice of awarding schedule contracts, with particular reference to the enormous cost overruns on section 15.

> It was let during Mr. Mackenzie's time, and in accordance with the schedule system which, we are sorry to say, is still being continued. No better illustration can be afforded of the evils of this system than is presented by the facts stated by our correspondent ["Thistle"]. Under it the contractor has no interest whatever in lessening the cost of the work,

for if he has fair schedule prices the more work he does the
better.[13]

The *Gazette* also lambasted Fleming for being in effect an absentee engineer
with his Ottawa headquarters far distant from the field operations and worse,
Fleming off in England.

Fleming was indignant, and vented his rage in a letter to Tupper.

> The Montreal *Gazette* is a government paper. The charges
> consequently have unusual weight. If they are true I should
> not, my staff should not, be permitted to hold office for a sin-
> gle hour. If they are not true why should a government organ
> urge them so persistently? As the papers may have escaped
> your notice I draw your attention to the libelous articles.[14]

Fleming was tempting fate.

The pro-Liberal Toronto *Globe* rushed to the defence of the old
Mackenzie administration and the schedule contract system. The *Globe*
noted in an editorial on 28 January:

> It is no matter for surprise that the Montreal *Gazette* should
> be engaged in an attempt to procure a change in the manner
> of letting public contracts. The schedule system now in
> force is one which gives a Minister like Sir Charles Tupper
> the fewest chances for collusion with contractors.[15]

The *Globe* argued that the controversial and costly section 15 vindicated the
schedule system.

> The case of Section 15 on the Thunder Bay branch is
> adduced to show the failure of the schedule system, but it
> really shows its success. The surveys being rapidly made, the
> depth of certain swamps was not ascertained before the con-
> tract was let. The result is not that the original estimate is
> largely exceeded but the country has paid only for value
> received. The filling in of the "muskegs" had to be done, no
> matter what system was in force. Had the work been taken
> on at a bulk sum the contractor would either have been
> ruined by paying for work done on behalf of the people, or
> he would have presented a huge claim for extras. Under the

schedule system he will get just what he is entitled to if it is
honestly worked. The worst feature of the "bulk sum" system is that it gives the Government power to ruin many
contractors or make their fortunes at pleasure. With the
Pacific Scandal Ministry in office, who can doubt that the
power would be used in order to obtain funds for party purposes? The fact that a prominent Conservative organ has
been set up to demand a change which would facilitate corruption shows that the Government thinks of going back to
a system of "plunder made easy".[16]

The *Gazette* opened a new avenue of attack on 10 February by calling
into question Fleming's judgement and motive in recommending that the
railway line cross the Red River at Selkirk rather than Winnipeg. Fleming
contended that Selkirk was a safer crossing point because of the danger of
spring floods and wash-outs at Winnipeg. Before the railway era Winnipeg
was the commercial centre of Manitoba because of its location at the conflu-
ence of the Assiniboine and Red Rivers. The Red River used to carry freight
from the United States, and Winnipeg became the principal distribution
point. Selkirk is north of Winnipeg. The *Gazette* was in no doubt that
Winnipeg was destined to become the leading city of the west, and that
Fleming and his district engineer, Mr. Rowan, by favouring Selkirk were
indifferent to this fact of life.

The newspapers continued their slanging match throughout the winter
of 1880; taken together with the acrimonious debate in the House of
Commons in April over the railway supply bill, and the serious fissures in
Conservative Party unity, the government had to do something. Galt's pro-
posal for a royal commission of inquiry into railways was adopted, and the
Tory caucus assured that Fleming would be offered a change of jobs.

Tupper was forced to bite the bullet: on 22 May he relieved his battle-
scarred friend of his duties as chief engineer of the Pacific Railway, replacing
him with Collingwood Schreiber. The government did its utmost to sugar-
coat the pill for the grievously offended Sandford Fleming – he was given
thirty thousand dollars in compensation for previously unpaid service, and
appointed consultant engineer to the government at six thousand dollars a
year. He was also named chief engineer of the Intercolonial Railway for the
purpose of investigating the several million dollars of unsettled claims arising from the construction phase. Fleming knew, however, that further association with government railway works would only keep alive the campaign
of vilification against him. The unsettled Intercolonial claims he was now
asked to investigate arose from the fixed price mileage system of contract let-

ting he had so strenuously opposed. Fleming wrote to Tupper on 11 June to decline the offer:

> I cannot be blind to the fact that my removal from the office of Engineer-in-Chief of the Pacific Railway had been brought about by pressure from certain quarters. The Montreal *Gazette* is the organ of those persons whence the pressure comes and judging from articles they appear still to be dissatisfied and may insist upon a further change. The tone of these articles is so virulent that it appears quite likely the persons referred to will follow up their hostility to me still further and as I would not wish to put the Government in the position of again yielding perhaps it would be better to cut the knot at once and sever my connection with the public service.[17]

Fleming had been tarred by his association with the Mackenzie administration and its half-hearted commitment to completing the transcontinental line. His undoing, however, was more complex than that; bound up with the endemic factionalism in the loose political alliances of the early post-Confederation years. First there was Mackenzie, who was motivated by his sense of justice to honour a commitment to British Columbia that he thought never should have been made, but who was constantly looking over his shoulder lest his party be torn asunder by disagreements over just how far the government should go to honour that commitment. Fleming marched to Mackenzie's tune; but not at the expense of his professional integrity; he did not, for example, favour Mackenzie's impractical railway-waterway combination, and he resisted it. If his health had permitted him to get out into the field more, and also to remain in closer touch with Mackenzie, damaging insubordination within the engineering branch might never have got out of hand.

Fleming certainly was no bookkeeper; with better support on the accounting and financial control side he might have been freed to devote himself more fully to the survey and engineering skills he knew best. As for his association with Tupper, for a variety of reasons various factions in the Conservative Party had it in for Tupper – some, perhaps, because of jealousy at his pre-eminent position in the party; others because of a desire to get the lucrative railway contract. Fleming's association with Mackenzie's railway policy was the chink in Tupper's armour the conspirators were looking for. Marcus Smith recognized this and used it cunningly to sow discord within the Conservative Party for his own purposes. Fleming, then, was in considerable measure the victim of circumstances beyond his control; he had been swept into the maelstrom of vicious political in-fighting. However, his long absences from duty, a lack of effective supervision over staff, and on occasion a wavering conviction ultimately made it impossible for him to withstand the assaults on his competence and integrity. The old mistrust that had begun with the Pictou Railway still stalked him.

Horseshoe trestle located a few kilometres west of Schreiber, c. 1884.
Canadian Pacific Archives, CP 12576

CPR construction in Fraser Valley, B.C., c. 1884.
Canadian Pacific Archives, 13561–2

The Métis uprising of 1885, led by Louis Riel, was decisively put down, owing in considerable measure to the effectiveness of the railway in moving forward troops (one of whom was Fleming's son Franky) within days of mobilization. At Riel's subsequent trial his lawyers pleaded insanity, but he was found guilty and sentenced to death. Meanwhile, a Parliament grateful to the CPR voted the extra funds so desperately needed to complete construction to the Pacific coast. Riel was hanged at Regina a week after the last spike was driven on the CPR.

National Archives of Canada, PA 27055

Bridge under construction in British Columbia, 1885. The enormous engineering and construction challenges of the transcontinental railway were nowhere more daunting than in the mountain barriers of British Columbia. The great burden of human and material resources marshalled to finish the job brought the Canadian Pacific Railway to the brink of financial ruin as late as spring 1885.

National Archives of Canada, C 1402

Building the railway through Kicking Horse Pass, 1885.
Glenbow Archives, Calgary, Alberta, NA–531–5

Railway construction camp at summit of Rogers Pass, 1885.
Glenbow Archives, Calgary, Alberta, NA–930–1

Laying track in British Columbia, 1885. The end was now in sight, thanks to funds
secured by a relief bill in Parliament in July 1885. There would be no denying
the CPR and Van Horne now.

National Archives of Canada, C 1602

Track maintenance on the Canadian Pacific Railway, c. 1885.
Canadian Pacific Archives, 19990

On the completion of the CPR through the Rockies, some employees drove a ceremonial
last spike near Donald, B.C., 7 November 1885.
Glenbow Archives, Calgary, Alberta, NA–548–1

On the morning of 7 November 1885, Donald Smith drove home the last spike on the CPR at Craigellachie in Eagle Pass, B.C. Around him stand Sandford Fleming (in top hat, over Smith's right shoulder); William Van Horne (to Smith's right, hands buried deep in his pockets); and a sampling of the thousands of surveyors, engineers, and labourers who brought the dream to life. Fleming called it "the moment of triumph." And so it was – the culmination of an epic political and engineering drama.

National Archives of Canada, C 11371

The first through train bound for the Pacific coast left Montreal on 28 June 1886.
Shown here two days later at Port Arthur, Ontario, it covered the 4,648 kilometres in 140
hours. By the end of December 1886 the government was estimated to have spent
$72 million on the CPR main line and $44.5 million on the Intercolonial, for a total of
$116.5 million, an enormous burden for the young, sparsely populated country.
National Archives of Canada, PA 144822

Prime Minister John A. Macdonald would have liked to be on the first through train to the Pacific coast when it left Montreal on 28 June 1886, but he was not able to leave his work until 10 July, when he, his wife, his secretary Joseph Pope, travelling companions and servants set out from the Ottawa station. The CPR general manager, Van Horne, laid on a special carriage, the "Jamaica," equipped even with mesh window screens to keep out the dust and mosquitoes. At last Macdonald was to see the western expanses he had brought into Canada, and from the vantage point of the transcontinental railway line he had been instrumental in bringing about. It was a triumphal progress. Pope recorded their arrival in Winnipeg: "Among the crowd gathered round the car was an enthusiastic young Tory who was cheering with all his might. Upon Sir John's appearance the enthusiasm became tremendous. When the lull came, the young Tory, who evidently had never seen Sir John before in his life, remarked in a low voice to a friend standing by, 'Seedy-looking old beggar, isn't he?' and then resumed his cheering with redoubled vigour, as though determined that his private impressions should not be allowed to interfere with his party loyalty."

Near Calgary, in Blackfoot country, Macdonald met the great Chief Crowfoot. The chief complained to Macdonald about the prairie fires caused by the railway engines, and pleaded for more food supplies for his people.

For long stretches through some of the most precarious passages in B.C.'s Rocky Mountains, Macdonald and his wife rode on the cowcatcher at the front of the engine. Pope had a near miss perched out front when the train struck a pig on the tracks, sending it flying in his direction.

Two weeks after setting out from Ottawa, Macdonald and his party reached Port Moody. They transferred to a steamer for Victoria, and after a three-week stay in the B.C. capital, they boarded the train again, arriving back in Ottawa on 31 August.

National Archives of Canada, C 24832

The final destination of the first transcontinental CPR train was Port Moody, B.C.
The CPR subsequently decided to extend the line to Granville, renamed Vancouver, further
down Burrard Inlet. This picture shows the arrival of the first CPR passenger train in
Vancouver on 23 May 1887. Three months later the CPR steamer *Abyssinia*, from
Hong Kong and Japan, docked at the wharf to the left of the picture, becoming
the first transpacific liner to connect with the CPR.

City of Vancouver Archives, CAN.P.78.N52

CPR passenger train with Engine 98, at Medicine Hat station, 1889.
Glenbow Archives, Calgary, Alberta, NA–967–13

Prime Minister Wilfrid Laurier in the Diamond Jubilee procession through the streets of London, 1897. Laurier championed a second transcontinental railway line to respond to the rapidly spreading settlement north of the CPR line. He spoke with great passion in introducing the Grand Trunk Pacific scheme in the House of Commons: "To those who urge upon us the policy of tomorrow, and tomorrow, and tomorrow; to those who tell us, wait, wait, wait; to those who advise us to pause, to consider, to reflect, to calculate and to inquire, our answer is: No, this is a time for action."

National Archives of Canada, C 28727

By 1899 the railway controversies were behind Fleming and the fight for the Pacific cable all but won. Here he is, surrounded by family in the conservatory at Winterholme, Ottawa, on Christmas Day, 1899.

National Archives of Canada, PA 66753

Max Aitken (later Lord Beaverbrook) had great business acumen; his merger plan to create the Canada Cement Company was only one example in a long career of mega-projects on both sides of the Atlantic. Aitken moved to London, England, in 1910, where, doubtless inspired by his friend, Canadian-born Andrew Bonar Law, he entered politics and won a seat for the Conservatives (Britain's only Canadian-born prime minister, Bonar Law was from New Brunswick, where Beaverbrook grew up). Beaverbrook established a chain of newspapers and became minister of aircraft production in Churchill's wartime government.

National Archives of Canada, C 47345

Sandford Fleming in later, but clearly still vigorous, life.
Canadian Pacific Archives, 5373

CHAPTER 10

WITCH HUNT

The Liberals were convinced that the announced royal commission to inquire into Pacific Railway affairs was a calculated witch hunt, intended to discredit the former Mackenzie government in advance of the next federal election. As far as the Toronto *Globe* was concerned, the proper imperative for the inquiry was growing evidence of Conservative government mismanagement and irregularities in the awarding of contracts. The *Globe* was certain that the composition of the three-man commission was deliberately stacked against the Liberals – George M. Clarke, an Ontario judge, Samuel Keefer, a civil engineer, and Edward Miall, assistant commissioner in the Inland Revenue Department.

There was good reason to suspect that Keefer and Miall had personal scores to settle with the former prime minister, Mackenzie. Keefer had been employed by a contractor to report favourably on a claim outstanding against the Liberal government; Mackenzie had dismissed Keefer's report with the assertion that it merely contained what he had been told to write by his employers. Keefer was appointed by the subsequent Conservative government to arbitrate another contractor's claim for work done on the Intercolonial, and Mackenzie objected to the award recommended by Keefer. Miall had served on a government board for which he was paid a salary, but he submitted a supplementary claim for extra work; the Mackenzie government granted Miall a more modest bonus than he expected; Miall later went after the Conservatives for increased compensation, to which Mackenzie strongly objected. As for the third commissioner, the *Globe* reported that, "Judge Clarke has probably no greater animosity against Mr. Mackenzie than any other bitter Tory, and will get up a case against him no more readily than any other partisan who hopes to find favour in the eyes of the powers that be."[1]

The royal commission was established in June 1880 to investigate allegations of neglect and other derelictions of duty by the officers and others employed on the CPR. Hearings began in Ottawa in August and continued for a year, with testimony from more than a hundred witnesses at sessions in Ottawa and Winnipeg, including assistant engineers from the engineering branch, contractors, Fleming's difficult deputies Horetzky and Smith, the present minister of railways, Charles Tupper, and the obdurate Alexander Mackenzie. Fleming, of course, would be a key witness, but to his chagrin he was not summoned until the following April, well after much damaging evidence against him had been heard. Indeed, all the evidence from all the witnesses reflected in one way or another on Fleming's performance – accounts of shameful extravagance, rampant patronage, and woeful confusion and dissension within the engineering department. The evidence paints an often disturbing picture of a great "national undertaking," and Fleming's major role in its execution.

Political patronage: Fleming described to the commission the difficulties he had encountered in assembling a competent and dedicated staff. At first it was hard to get competent men because they were employed on the Intercolonial and then, the political patronage system had to be obliged. The various regions of the country had to be considered in making appointments; different nationalities and creeds had to be consulted. Worse still, Fleming had no latitude to fire incompetents; if he felt that an employee hired through political influence simply had to go, he was obliged to consult the minister. The commission put it squarely to Fleming:

> I wish to get your opinion, on this point: whether you believe, from your experience in the management of the Canadian Pacific Railway, that the public interest had suffered on account of the patronage being in the hands of a political party from time to time?

Fleming replied laconically, "No doubt of it."[2]

Extravagant spending: Witnesses gave a great many examples of wasteful spending, with no adequate financial management system in the engineering branch; Fleming was paymaster and bookkeeper as well as chief engineer. He said he knew there were abuses, but pleaded they invariably came to his attention too late. Fleming believed that the work could have been done for much less by a private company. As the testimony grew more damaging Fleming began to mention names; he fingered the extravagances of Moberly in British Columbia, specifically an exorbitant purchase of supplies for an exploration of the Howse Pass even after he had been ordered to abandon operations there. Moberly's purchases, according to Fleming, included gold pens and quicksilver; Moberly wrote later that Fleming had got it wrong – it was gold pans, not pens, and quicksilver for prospecting along the survey lines to determine the value of the land.

Horetzky told shocking stories of wild extravagance, but his testimony was so coloured by vindictiveness and spite that no one knew when to believe him. According to Horetzky it was customary for American traders on the west coast to buy mules from the survey crews at $4 or $5 each and resell them to the government at $200 after fattening them up. He also told of squandered supplies in the survey camps:

> At one camp I saw a case of Hennessey's brandy, and saw the ground laid out with pudding, and ham, and bacon, and sugar and supplies, in the most extravagant manner possible, for Indians and men – canned fruits and canned turkeys in the camp – and I have seen the engineer drunk. I saw him drunk that night, and I was told by his men he went to bed drunk regularly.[3]

Surveys: The commission spent much of its time examining the manner in which surveys were ordered and carried out; particular attention was paid to the survey work on sections 13–15 from Lake Superior to the Prairies. The surveys in this region were found to be wholly inadequate – grossly inaccurate estimates resulted in enormous cost over-runs, particularly in the vast muskeg region; they were surveyed in winter when the ground was frozen, so there was no accurate assessment of the road bed or the quantity of solid landfill available for embankments. Mackenzie hewed to his story that he had been the unwitting dupe of Fleming's bad advice. Fleming gave the commission an entirely different version of events. He spoke of the government's desire to get construction moving as quickly as possible, and Mackenzie confirmed that this was the case, at least as far as the Red River line was concerned. In saying so, however, Mackenzie betrayed his lack of commitment to an unbroken railway line, telling the commission that his government's policy was to obtain the best and shortest link between Thunder Bay and Red River; they had considered not proceeding with the line east of Thunder Bay for many years, using instead the waterways as the means of communication between the Ontario railway system and Fort William, and possibly also utilizing the small lakes in the interior of the country for a time. The government might, perhaps, have chosen not to commence any building at all until the entire line was surveyed, Mackenzie said, but believed some construction had to proceed.

Marcus Smith was uncharacteristically subdued in his testimony. He stuck to one essential point, that as Fleming's deputy he was faithful to his chief's views, even in the latter's absence – the implication being that Fleming was solely to blame for any mistakes. According to Smith, soundings should have been made of the muskeg region before construction began. Not surprisingly, he had more to say about the battle of the routes, and censured Fleming yet again for excluding his map from the 1878 report. Horetzky was more bitter still about Fleming's apparent refusal to consider any but the Yellowhead–Burrard Inlet route; in classic Horetzky style the caustic-tongued engineer sputtered:

> Mr. Fleming stands condemned of deliberate and malicious falsehood. His malevolence has been directed against me ever since I brought the Pine Pass under his notice. In doing so I unconsciously wounded his vanity, which could not brook the idea of anyone but himself proposing a route.[4]

Red River Crossing: There was much testimony concerning Fleming's recommendation to bridge the Red River at Selkirk and not at Winnipeg, which to many seemed the more obvious location. Fleming's choice was based on two factors. First, from the engineering point of view the crossing at Selkirk made more sense because the Red River at Winnipeg was subject to serious spring flooding, so that a bridge there ran the risk of being washed away. The facile answer was to build a higher bridge, but Fleming pointed out the increased costs of that option. Second, Fleming took into account the fact that the government owned a large tract of land at Selkirk, which would increase in value if a town were established there. "I considered Winnipeg of importance," he said, "but not of sufficient importance to twist the main line out of its particular course to reach it."[5] But Fleming's detractors would not be satisfied; not when Winnipeg so obviously was Manitoba's city of the future. There were whispers inevitably that Fleming might have had a personal interest in the Selkirk location, but he put such rumours to rest – he owned no private land in Manitoba, he said. His only private interest in the whole of the Northwest was his shares in the Hudson's Bay Company.

Rail purchases: During the summer of 1874 the word from England was of a great fall in the price of steel rails – it had dropped from £18 per ton to £10, and stayed there for six months. Fleming was in direct touch with steel companies in England, and all signs were that the price of steel rails had bottomed out and would soon start to rise. In August 1874 Fleming recommended to Mackenzie that they should take advantage of the situation before it was too late; Mackenzie agreed and authorized the purchase of 50,000 tons at the low £10 price. But Fleming and Mackenzie had misjudged on two counts – the prices kept falling after the purchase contracts were signed to an ultimate low of £4. 10s. in 1879, and when the huge shipment arrived there was no immediate use for it, so far behind had the construction schedule fallen – in fact the first construction did not begin for nearly a year after the rails were ordered. Eleven thousand tons went to the Intercolonial; the remainder were left to rust for lack of use. The commissioners were not satisfied, and probed to learn more. Why had the government been in such a hurry to bring in the massive quantity of rails? Neither Fleming nor Mackenzie was convincing in his testimony; both said they had been anxious for construction to begin and it was, therefore, important to sustaining momentum to have the construction materials at hand. What went wrong then? According to Fleming, "there was a great deal of hesitation about the beginning of the works through some cause or other, partly political, if my recollection is correct."[6] So in the end the argument came back to the Liberal government's half-hearted commitment to the project.

Management of the engineering department: The commissioners wanted to know what controls there were in the engineering department over the conduct of operations and, in particular, the accounting procedures for such large expenditures. From the first day of hearings it was apparent that in all things except recruitment Fleming had had a virtually free hand. When he was required to refer to the minister his expert opinion usually prevailed, simply because he knew more about surveying and railway construction than his political masters did. The root of the management disarray appears to have been the government's failure when it appointed Fleming to lay down clear, written guidelines about the conduct of business in the engineering department, and the respective authority of the various levels of administration. Proceeding, then, with nothing more than a general mandate to get on with the job, Fleming made it up as he went along. He told the commission that his first self-ordained duty had been to gain a knowledge of the country, most of which was unknown, but he had to work fast since he was informed that construction had to begin within two years. Accordingly, except in the Prairies, Fleming dispensed with preliminary surveys and proceeded with the detailed instrumental surveys from the outset. If time had permitted, he testified, he would have started with exploratory surveys, which in the end would have saved a great deal of money.

Fleming had too little control over his far-flung engineering staff, and he did not go into the field as often as might have been expected; instead he wrote his reports to the government from the comfort of his office in Ottawa, basing them on field reports sent in by the assistant engineers. In the early years his life was complicated by the competing demands of the Intercolonial construction, but his extended absences from Ottawa from 1876 on had contributed greatly to the drift in his office. Marcus Smith had antagonized the government with his bull-headed promotion of his preferred western route; Mackenzie had ordered him dismissed but he refused to budge – it was an extraordinary and quite impossible situation.

The commission completed its hearings in September 1881 and submitted its report to Parliament the following April, just two months before the federal election. Almost every one of the 496 pages of conclusions contains a damning indictment of Fleming's performance. The commissioners concluded that there had been a great lack of business capacity in the management of resupply for the field crews; the commissary staff seemed unequal to the task, perhaps because of incompetent political appointees, and there was no adequate control over expenditures, which had been entrusted entirely to Fleming and his staff. The commissioners severely criticized Fleming's judgement in commencing with costly instrumental surveys instead of exploratory work first. Marcus Smith managed to come out on the side of the angels, in spite of the inordinate delays and expense he had caused by his insistent advocacy of the Pine Pass–Bute Inlet route long after it had been rejected by the government. Alexander Mackenzie was apportioned his share of the blame for delays and needless expenditure; the commission felt his insistence on examining a combined rail and waterway route had been a complete waste of time.

Most of the blame for the cost over-runs on sections 13–15 was laid at Fleming's feet; the commissioners concluded that he had failed to survey the region adequately, or to report clearly to the government the actual state of play. The cost over-runs were staggering, on one particular contract $1 million over the $1.5 million estimate. In some cases embankments were made through waters when only the depth of the water was known; often the lake and river bottoms were of soft mud and the embankments simply sank under the waters. The commissioners considered Fleming's choice of Selkirk over Winnipeg as the crossing-point of the Red River a mistake. It should have been evident, they said, that Winnipeg was destined to become an important distribution centre – the result of work carried out on the basis of Fleming's recommendation was a further loss of a half million dollars. If Fleming was considered hasty in his recommendations on the line between Lake Superior and Red River, he was found to be too slow in locating the line in other regions, partly because of his decision to begin with full-scale, time-consuming instrument surveys, when a quick exploratory survey would have sufficed. The long delay in settling on a West coast terminus was also deplored, particularly since Fleming waited until the end of 1876 to seek the opinion of the Admiralty on the Pacific coast harbours.

The commission findings were kinder to Fleming's field staff than to himself.

> It has been our duty to animadvert unfavourably in several
> instances, upon the engineering branch of the Department
> of Public Works having charge of the Surveying operations.
> It is with pleasure that we state that, during construction,

the engineers have shown ability, zeal, and the strictest integrity in the supervision of the work. The evidence shows that they fought inch by inch, and day by day, against what they thought to be attempted encroachments on the part of the contractors' engineers. We have felt that their determination to maintain the rights entrusted to their keeping, has in some cases led them to a strained construction of the specifications adverse to the contractors. Appeals were more than once made to the Chief Engineer or other superior officer by the contractor, which resulted in an interpretation more favourable to the contractor than the resident engineer was willing, without such authority to allow.[7]

In fairness to Fleming, the commissioners allowed that too often he had been hindered by circumstances not of his own making; for example, he had to wait for Parliament to vote the necessary monies before settling on the season's work – so spring often was well advanced before work could begin. Then there was the political patronage system, which hung like a millstone about Fleming's neck. The commissioners commented:

Considering the tenor of the evidence, and the fact that instrumental surveys were frequently undertaken, where, in our view of the evidence they might have been better omitted, we find it difficult to repress the suspicion that various staffs having been filled from the influence thus described by Mr. Fleming, work was sometimes invented for their occupation, as an alternative less embarrassing than ending their employment.[8]

They agreed completely with Fleming that the job could have been done with greater efficiency and economy as a private undertaking.

By far the greatest part of the commission's conclusions was taken up with a detailed examination of the contracts on the Pacific Railway. Of the seventy-two contracts, forty were let under Mackenzie, and the remainder under Tupper. The commissioners concluded that fifteen of Mackenzie's contracts were let in a manner that gave unfair advantage to contractors; no irregularities were found in the contracts let by Tupper. In some cases the commission reported outright collusion among tenderers in the interest of ensuring the lower tenders would be withdrawn. There were attempts also to influence members of Parliament to secure advantages in the letting of contracts. While Fleming was expected to report on all tenders, he fared badly on contracts for

50,000 tons of rails in 1874; the commission identified a number of irregular-ities – tenders advertised for only 5,000 tons with the vastly inflated quanti-ties decided on later, no order-in-council authorizing the calling of tenders, tenders not mentioning the Pacific Railway for fear of pushing up prices. There was no adequate explanation why such large quantities of rails were ordered when the Thunder Bay–Red River portion required less than 10,000 tons. In fact, in 1876 only 2,300 tons were used, for 40.8 kilometres of track laid westward from Fort William. Clearly there had been no pressing need for 50,000 tons; in the commissioners' view the only explanation of Fleming's precipitate action in buying huge quantities of rails was that he was in too much of a hurry to get construction moving. Lastly, there was the enormous burden placed on Fleming with his time and energies dissipated for five years between the Intercolonial and the Pacific Railway, making it extremely diffi-cult for him to spend much time in the field and weakening his health. "In our judgement this officer was overtaxed," the commissioners concluded.[9]

The commission findings were open to different interpretations, particu-larly coming only two months before a federal election. The Conservative Montreal *Gazette*'s headline on 12 April 1882 read: "Contract-Letting Under the Liberal Regime and What It Has Cost the Country." The Liberal Toronto *Globe* carried a different headline the following day, "A Carefully Compiled Tory Campaign Volume – Evidence of Tory Jobbery Glossed Over Endeavours to Revive Slanders Against Mr. Mackenzie."

The commission's report was a cruel blow to Fleming, who was still smarting from the sting of his dismissal from the CPR; it was, "unfair, ungen-erous and unjust," he wrote to Tupper, and to the prime minister:

> The report of the Pacific Railway Royal Commission brought before Parliament a few days ago is to a large extent a bill of indictment against myself. The accusations are for the most part implied but they are sufficiently definite to convey the impression that I am guilty of causing the waste of large sums of public money.[10]

Tupper encouraged Fleming to set out, in a letter, his considered comments on the royal commission findings, and arranged for them to be tabled in Parliament. Fleming's letter is a profound reply to the commission's serious indictment of his performance. He was convinced that the commission had been one-sided and biased against him, suppressing his evidence on many of the issues. Fleming knew he had been made the scapegoat of successive administrations:

Partisans expected that when the Government changed, I should change too and join them in traducing the previous Administration. I declined to lend myself to party. It only concerned me to act for the best under all circumstances, and loyally uphold the acts of the Department ... When the present party came into power the same experience was repeated; it was intensified by the fact that the previous Administration had the Pacific Railway under control for five years, while their predecessors had it for only two. It became my duty, as chief executive officer, to defend the acts of the Department under the Reform Administration. I was prepared to serve the new Administration as faithfully as the past, but I could not turn round and calumniate those I had previously served. Hence, a bitter feeling arose against me among some of the supporters of the present Government, which with concurrent circumstances of less importance, brought matters to a culmination ... A reader of the Report of the Commission without knowledge of the facts, could come only to one conclusion, viz: that three successive Administrations had employed a man to conduct the heaviest works ever undertaken by Canada, whose one aim and object was to do everything the way in which it should not be done.[11]

The greater part of Fleming's letter dealt with the specific indictments of his conduct. He acknowledged that the first sections had been hurriedly, possibly too hurriedly, placed under contract, but recalled that there had been great pressure to get the construction under way; a political necessity. As for the Red River crossing, Fleming said that subsequent events had proved his case against Winnipeg, with two bridges across the Red River, one of them at Winnipeg, having been swept away by floods. He was unrepentant about the massive rail purchase, claiming that universal opinion at the time favoured the deal and it was only circumstances beyond his control that prevented their early use. Fleming concluded:

The Commissioners condemn the Engineer-in-Chief, but in doing so they simply condemn the Government whose servant he was. They condemn three Administrations whose wishes he consulted, and whose instructions he carried out. They pay no regard to the state of things which existed ten years ago, nor to the political circumstances which dictated operations at that period and every subsequent year. It is obvious from the few facts which I submit, that the three gentlemen appointed on the 16th June, 1880, have not properly, and with becoming dignity, performed the duties of a Royal Commission.[12]

The Conservative government had in fact received very gentle treatment from the royal commission: although the commissioners' mandate was to consider all aspects of the Pacific Railway from its inception in 1871, a great deal was missing. There was no mention, for example, of Macdonald's hasty selection of the western terminus on Vancouver Island, long before surveys were complete; also overlooked was the failure of Macdonald's government to lay a single kilometre of track within the two-year start-up time promised to British Columbia. Nor were contract irregularities the sole purview of the Grits – Tupper, for example, awarded a contract for a section of the Pacific Railway between Port Moody and Emory Bar, British Columbia, to Andrew Onderdonk, a wealthy American contractor, although the tender was $210,000 higher than the lowest bid; yet Tupper got off scot-free in the commission report (he claimed a technicality for rejecting the lowest bid).

The commission was a whitewash of the Conservatives, and a tarring of the opposition Liberals, just before the federal election. Fleming was the lightning rod for the government's attack against Mackenzie and the Liberals.

There were few to stand by Fleming during this, his darkest hour; the wounds of these two years never completely healed. In 1898, nearly two decades after his dismissal from the Pacific Railway, Fleming wrote a deeply personal and revealing letter to his friend George Grant; the occasion was the publication of a book, *New Cyclopedia of Canada,* by Castle Hopkins, which all but erased Fleming's name from its reference to the Pacific Railway. The *Cyclopedia,* completely disregarding six years of construction during Fleming's tenure as chief engineer, stated that the first sod for the CPR had been turned in 1881. Fleming unburdened himself to Grant:

> I write with some warmth I am aware, and always with more candour to you than to any one else the more especially on this subject. We came near each other for many days on the two transcontinental journeys 26 and 15 years ago.
>
> I could not thus have concealed from you, if I had wished, the pride I felt in connection with this great national work while I remained in the prominent position I occupied as chief officer of the Government. I gave the best nine

or ten years of my life and unsparingly night and day my concentrated efforts to the Pacific Railway. I satisfied myself with the firm belief that I was serving my country in the way I could serve it best. I confess to you as to do so it relieves me some disappointments that my labours and my enthusiasm are already forgotten or ignored. I further confess that it was the greatest wrench of my life to separate myself from a service to which I had given all my powers so long with intense earnestness. I hope the pride I took in my work did not proceed wholly from vanity. I indulged the impression that I was performing a duty to my country which would stand a chance of not being soon forgotten – vain delusion – as the last literary production shows what shadows we are and what shadows we follow![13]

Grant offered to write to the Toronto papers to point out the *Cyclopedia's* gross distortion of the facts; Fleming suggested instead a note in the *Queen's Quarterly.* In the end, neither was done, and the record was uncorrected. Only the hurt remained.

CHAPTER 11

FINISHING THE JOB

Prime Minister John A. Macdonald wrote to Prof. Goldwin Smith on 7 July 1880:

> I am off for England on Saturday, with two of my colleagues. We have three substantial offers for the CPR – not only to build but to run it as a railway company, and to give satisfactory guarantees. So I confidently expect to relieve the country of all uncertainty as to cost, and to retain enough land to recoup Canada for expenditure up to this time.[1]

Three days later Macdonald, Tupper, and the agriculture minister, Joseph Pope, set off for England; in London they met with the president of the Grand Trunk Railway, Sir Henry Tyler, but he was not interested in pursuing the project so long as it was a condition that the line be carried along the difficult terrain of Lake Superior. The second offer, by the Earl of Dunmore, representing the London financial house of Puleston, Brown and Company, fell through. This left a mainly Canadian group alone in the field.

The Canadian offer came from a syndicate headed by Duncan McIntyre, of the Canada Central Railway, and George Stephen, who with his cousin Donald A. Smith was connected with the St. Paul, Minneapolis and Manitoba Railway. Smith stayed well in the background during the contract negotiations: he had been in bad odour with Macdonald ever since deserting him over the Pacific Scandal. Smith had run for Parliament in the 1878 election and won, but charges of bribery and corruption in the courts led to the election result being declared void in 1880 (he returned to the Commons in 1887). The syndicate kept very quiet about Smith's involvement, not wishing it to be known until every possible concession had been granted.

McIntyre travelled on the same ship carrying the government representatives to England in July. On 14 September an agreement was signed in London by Macdonald, Tupper, and David Macpherson for the government, and by McIntyre, the London financial house of Morton, Rose and Company, and a German-French financial group, Kohn, Reinach and

Company. The contract was drawn up by John Abbott, who had been Sir Hugh Allan's solicitor, and was now to become counsel for the CPR.

The Canadians were back home within a week of signing, once again with McIntyre in tow; the contract was signed on 21 October and put before Parliament in December; debate on the contract lasted more than two months. Blake, who was now the Liberal leader, thought to build the railroad on the terms proposed was utter folly; his party favoured a line as far as Sault Ste. Marie, another line across the Prairies, and use of American lines south of Lake Superior to connect the two. The CPR bill passed on 11 February, and the CPR was incorporated a few days later.

George Stephen had begun his career as a draper's assistant in Aberdeen; he emigrated from Scotland to Canada in 1850, and rose to become president of the Bank of Montreal. His cousin Donald A. Smith worked his way up the Hudson's Bay Company ladder to become its senior executive and governor in Canada. Stephen and Smith had some experience with running a railway; some years before, Smith had persuaded his cousin, along with two other financiers, to put up the money to buy the St. Paul, Minneapolis and Manitoba Railway as a speculative venture. They tried to interest Fleming in becoming a partner in the venture. Stephen and Smith set about to reorganize the ailing company, and in time succeeded in realizing a handsome profit from it. The two cousins were extremely generous with their wealth; they gave large gifts to McGill University, and sufficient funds to establish the Royal Victoria Hospital in Montreal. Smith became chancellor of McGill, and both men were knighted, in recognition of their services. Smith became Lord Strathcona, and Stephen was given the title Lord Mount Stephen.

Smith encouraged his more cautious financier cousin to make a bid for the big Canadian Pacific Railway contract. Stephen was won over by the favourable terms offered; the CPR received a cash grant of $25 million and 10.1 million hectares of land. The government transferred ownership to the new company of the portion of line already completed between Fort William and Winnipeg, and the Pembina branch line south from Winnipeg to the United States border. It was further agreed that the government would be responsible for construction of the costly section from the Pacific coast to Kamloops. There would be no taxes on CPR property and no customs duties on imported construction materials; most important, the company would enjoy a monopoly of western railway traffic for the next twenty years. Stephen resigned his position as chief executive of the Bank of Montreal to become the first president of the CPR; D.L. McIntyre became vice-president. R.B. Agnes, general manager of the bank, also became a member of the CPR's executive committee. The continued close association of the executive with the Bank of Montreal meant it was particularly well placed to secure the necessary financial backing.

If Smith was the prime mover, and Stephen represented the money, William Cornelius Van Horne was the brains and the muscle behind the execution of the project. The thirty-eight-year-old general superintendent of the Chicago, Milwaukee and St. Paul Railroad had extensive railway experience during the era of great expansion in the United States; if anyone could complete the CPR with the minimum of delay it was this man, with his prodigious energy, boldness, and apparently endless capacity for hard work. A contemporary wrote of Van Horne that "he seems to be ubiquitous, passing quickly from Montreal to the Pacific, and turning up in Boston or New York or St. John, N.B. or Quebec with the rapidity of a bird."[2] Van Horne took charge in Winnipeg on 2 January 1882, and had soon put together an enthusiastic and talented team, dedicated to finishing the job well within the ten years stipulated in the contract.

The construction crews kept up a feverish pace; on forty-two consecutive working days in August and September of 1882 they laid an average 5.02 kilometres of track per day; in July and August 1883, on forty-eight consecutive days, it was 5.54 kilometres a day and on two single days an astonishing 7.63 and 10.21 kilometres respectively. By the end of November 1883 they had reached Kicking Horse Pass in the Rockies.

Fleming's recommendations were scrapped, and the surveys conducted under his direction discarded. The CPR favoured running the line in a more southerly direction; the fertility of the soil in the southern portions of the Prairies was known and attractive to settlers, while the area farther north, along Fleming's proposed line, was a more doubtful proposition – especially in the east, where there were large tracts of marshland. With the southern route there was also the interesting possibility of capturing some of the traffic that was currently being siphoned off by American railways just south of the border. The CPR's twenty-year monopoly assured the company that there need be no fear of competing Canadian lines probing south to connect with American lines for the foreseeable future. Already Tupper had taken the line across the Red River at Winnipeg instead of at Selkirk, and laid track in the direction of Brandon, well south of Fleming's proposed line via the narrows of Lake Manitoba.

The Yellowhead Pass now was too far north to be practicable, and it became clear that another passage through the Rockies would have to be found. While a southerly route would be shorter, the mountain barrier in the south was far more daunting. The secretary of the CPR Company wrote to Tupper in December 1881 concerning the Yellowhead Pass:

I have the honour at the direction of the Board to inform you, that there is a great probability that a passage through the Rocky Mountains will be discovered which will afford a much more direct and shorter communication with Kamloops than could be obtained by means of the route by the Yellowhead Pass, in which case it would doubtless be in the interest, both of the Government and the Company, to carry the line by such improved route.[3]

Tupper replied that he wanted to know what new passage was being proposed before relieving the company of its commitment to proceed by the Yellowhead. Van Horne favoured the Kicking Horse Pass, but beyond it lay the forbidding Selkirk Range, which the railway would also have to traverse.

Fleming had returned to England in October 1882 in the wake of the humiliation of the royal commission report; its scathing conclusions seemed to have made his position in railway circles completely untenable. By now, as well, he had other fish to fry; matters on both sides of the Atlantic and around the world occupied his attention. He was intent on promoting a submarine telegraph cable from Canada across the floor of the Pacific Ocean to Australia, the universal standard time movement also required careful nurturing, and since 1880 he had been chancellor of Queen's College at Kingston.

Fleming's expertise in railway surveys and engineering was, however, too great to be written off so easily. In June 1883 he received a telegram from George Stephen, asking him for his assistance in British Columbia as soon as possible. Fleming had only been in London three days, having just arrived with his daughter, Minnie, but he quickly made arrangements to return, and after a month in the United Kingdom he sailed for Canada.

Fleming arrived in Rimouski and took the Intercolonial to Halifax; on 9 August, after a few days there, he started for the west. He arranged for his son, Sandford Jr., to join him in Toronto, and the two met George Grant in Winnipeg, for a second trek to the Pacific. A decade had passed since his first great march across the mountains; Fleming now was fifty-six years old. He met with the CPR directors in Montreal to discuss the terms of reference; Stephen and Van Horne wanted Fleming's opinion on a proposed route through the Selkirks. A possible opening had been discovered the year before by Major A.B. Rogers, an American railway surveyor hired by the CPR to investigate the southern passes, but Fleming was the acknowledged expert, and could verify the practicability of the proposed pass. They also wanted Fleming to inspect the section between Kamloops and Port Moody, which was being constructed by the federal government; Stephen suspected it was not being built to CPR standards, despite government protestations to the contrary. Fleming later confirmed that the contractor, Andrew Onderdonk, was skimping on specifications, and a protracted arbitration followed.

Fleming was on excellent terms with his old friends Donald Smith and George Stephen; he had met Smith when he and George Grant stopped at Smith's Hudson's Bay Company headquarters outside Winnipeg in 1872, and they had been friends ever since. Fleming was appointed to the board of directors of the Hudson's Bay Company in 1882. Smith, Stephen, and Fleming were keen fishermen, and visited each other's fishing camps up and down the Matapedia and Restigouche rivers every summer, where they discussed the fur trade and railway matters.

Sandford Jr. joined his father in Toronto, and after a visit with Fleming's mother in Collingwood they boarded a steamer on 14 August for the journey to Port Arthur at the head of the Lakes. At Port Arthur they took the train for the 752-kilometre journey to Winnipeg. While unbroken, the line was still far from complete. Many station buildings were yet to be constructed; at such stops, breakfast was served under a large canvas awning set up along the tracks. At another place, the train passed the graves of workmen who had died through careless handling of nitro-glycerine explosives. After twenty-four hours the train steamed into Winnipeg, now a bustling city of 30,000; Fleming and his son were met on the station platform by George Grant. A violent rainstorm raged that night; trees were torn up, buildings unroofed and a church steeple thrown down. The streets of Winnipeg were turned into a sea of deep black treacle-like mud, as Fleming, Grant, and Sandford Jr. carried their bags, blankets, waterproofs, saddles, bridles, and tents to the train. Fleming arranged with the chief commissioner of the Hudson's Bay Company at Winnipeg to have supplies sent from the company establishment in British Columbia, to await them at a point east of Kamloops; the supplies were to reach the Columbia River opposite the Eagle Pass by 8 or 10 September.

There were certain advantages to making the journey in the employ of the CPR; Fleming's party travelled from Winnipeg in a private car at the rear of a train consisting of four railway cars, a baggage car, and a post office car. Their private coach was complete with kitchen and cook: a far cry from their journey across the Prairies a decade earlier! The train sped by the several settlements growing up now along the line – Portage la Prairie, Brandon, Regina, Moose Jaw. At Swift Current the train picked up a number of construction cars. The railway was still a novelty to the Plains Indians, and they gathered at station stops for a closer look.

> At some of the stations there are groups of Indians, men and women. We enter into a conversation with them through an interpreter on the platform. Pie-a-Pot, the great Indian

chief, we are told, has gone on a mission to the Lieutenant-Governor at Regina to complain of the smoke of the loco-motive, which he considers to be an evil medicine to ruin the health of his people … What will be the fate of the Indian as the plains are filled up? Is he to be engulfed in the common field of industry? Is he to become civilized and labour with the rest of us at the prosaic occupations of every day life? Is he to be uncared for and left to his fate, or be clothed and fed in idleness? The problem is not an easy one to unravel. I learned from one of the passengers, who seems to speak with authority, that at present some ten thousand Indians receive an allowance of rations. It may be said that the Indian territory has been appropriated in the interest of the community, and that it is a consequent duty to care for the Red man. If it be possible the course to follow is to train the coming generation to habits of industry, and self-reliance. Is it possible?[4]

Qu'Appelle passed by, then Medicine Hat; Indian ponies chased the train as it steamed and belched its way westward. The Rockies loomed into view. There now were twenty loaded cars on the train, and the locomotive was labouring. Finally they arrived at the western limit of the line, Calgary. The road from here to Kamloops, on the far side of the Rockies and Selkirk ranges, would be difficult; there was a wagon road for some distance up the valley of the Bow River, then a trail passable on horseback. Finally, they would cross the Selkirks on foot. In Calgary, Fleming and his party complet-ed arrangements made at Winnipeg to have supplies waiting at the Columbia River, and bought pack horses and food supplies at the Hudson's Bay Company store.

Fleming, Grant, and young Sandford left Calgary on 23 August; barely a kilometre out of town they were delayed for an hour at the ferry crossing of the Bow River. A few minutes later a wheel came off the wagon and had to be repaired. And so the expedition made for the mountains – the lead wagon, followed by the baggage wagon, pack horses, riding horses, and a half-dozen packers strung out behind. The way grew more difficult as they began the ascent into the mountains. Along the way they met CPR engineering crews encamped, or at work locating a route through the valley of the Kicking Horse River. Soon the wagons were left behind and the baggage transferred to the pack horses, but the animals had great difficulty. There was little graz-ing pasture for them in the mountains, and the footing was treacherous:

> We cross clay, rock and gravel slides at a giddy height. To look down gives one an uncontrollable dizziness to make the head swim and the view unsteady, even with men of tried nerve. I do not think that I can ever forget that terrible walk; it was the greatest trial I ever experienced. We are from five to eight hundred feet high [151–242 m] on a path of from ten to fifteen inches [35 cm] wide and at some points almost obliterated, with slopes above and below us so steep that a stone would roll into the torrent in the abyss below. There are no trees or branches or twigs which we can grip to aid us in our advance on the narrow, precarious footing.[5]

Five kilometres from the mouth of the Kicking Horse Valley, they met, by prearrangement, Major Rogers in company with a Major Hurd, and here they had their first unobstructed view of the Selkirk Range. The Kicking Horse Valley turns into the valley of the Columbia River at this point. They continued on to Rogers' camp. The Rockies had been traversed, and they could now, if they chose, pass round the Selkirks by descending the Columbia as far as Boat Encampment, and then going on by way of Eagle Pass through the Gold Range to Kamloops; but their mission was to investigate the pass Rogers claimed to have discovered through the Selkirks. Rogers proposed to accompany Fleming part of the way, and to send his nephew, Albert Rogers, with them over the entire route. For the next portion of their journey they would follow the Columbia River in a northwesterly direction for fifty-one kilometres on the way to Boat Encampment, and then turn west to enter the Selkirks by the valley of the Beaver River, leading to an opening in the west of the range. Once the summit was crossed, they would descend the valley of the Illecillewaet River in a southwesterly direction to the Columbia River, directly opposite Eagle Pass.

The party rested in Rogers' camp on Sunday 1 September; twenty-two in all were present at Grant's worship service. The horses were sent on ahead, to be joined the following day by Fleming and his party, who proceeded first by canoe down the Columbia River, then on foot along the Beaver River for twenty-four kilometres. Finally, they ascended a branch of the river, known as Beaver Creek, to the summit of Rogers Pass. Fleming carried a box of cigars to mark the occasion.

> We have no wine, so we can only congratulate Major Rogers over the cigars on the discovery of a pass so far practicable and on certain conditions appearing to furnish a solution of the problem of crossing over the Selkirk range instead of

making a detour – following the Columbia by the Boat Encampment. We are now 4,600 feet [1,390 m] above the sea, surrounded by mountains of all forms, pyramidal, conical and serrated.[6]

Rogers was indebted to a report by Walter Moberly for the tip that had led him to the examination of the Bear Creek passage through the Selkirks. Moberly had been the first European to ascend the Illecillewaet River after his discovery of the Eagle Pass eighteen years before, when he was engaged in explorations for the government of British Columbia. In his report, Moberly referred to a branch of the Illecillewaet that he had not had the time to explore; it was this branch that Rogers pursued to success.

Fleming and his party were euphoric at finding themselves at the summit of the Selkirks.

As we view the landscape we feel as if some memorial should be preserved of our visit here, and we organize a Canadian Alpine Club. The writer, as a grandfather, is appointed interim president, Dr. Grant, secretary, and my son, Sandford Hall Fleming, treasurer. A meeting was held and we turn to one of the springs rippling down to the Illecillewaet and drink success to the organization. Unanimously we carry resolutions of acknowledgement to Major Rogers, the discoverer of the pass, and to his nephew for assisting him. The summit on which we stand is a dry meadow about a mile in extent, with excellent grass. On the approaches we found raspberries, blackberries, blueberries, pigeonberries and gooseberries. They were a treat to us with our hard fare. Fruit, gathered from the bush is always more pleasant to the taste, and fancy eating these delicious fruits in the heart of the Selkirk Range, nearly a vertical mile above the ocean! We are in the best of health, and have the digestion of ostriches. The air is bracing, the day fine. We have regained our freshness and elasticity, and to show that we are all still young and unaffected by our journey we deem it proper to go through a game of leap-frog, about the only amusement at our command, an act of Olympic worship to the deities in the heart of the Selkirks![7]

Started now on the descent of the western side of the Selkirks, they moved down the Illecillewaet past a conical peak they named Syndicate Peak.

"Major Rogers declared it would be the summit of his ambition to plant on its highest point the Union Jack on the day that the first through train passed along the gorge we were now travelling."[8] Rogers now parted company with Fleming to return to his camp. The back of the journey had been broken; they arrived at the Columbia River again, and boarded a steamer at Shuswap Lake to continue on along the Thompson River to Kamloops.

Fleming had seen for himself the pass through the Selkirks, and reported from Kamloops to CPR head office in Montreal that the route by way of the Kicking Horse and Rogers passes was practicable. Notwithstanding, Fleming never departed from his own long-held opinion that the Yellowhead would have been the best route from a strictly engineering point of view. Fleming, Grant, and Sandford Jr. returned to the east by way of California and the American railway system. A year later Fleming's account of his second great trip across the continent was published as *England and Canada – A Summer Tour between Old and New Westminster*.

The Canadian Pacific Railway Company ran into serious financial difficulties by late 1883; it was unable to sell its stock or land grant bonds, or otherwise raise the money it needed to carry on with construction. There was a great rivalry between the CPR and the Grand Trunk Railway in the east, where the GTR had a virtual monopoly in southern Ontario – the GTR feared the CPR's intrusion into the region it had for so long dominated, and used its great influence in London to frustrate efforts to secure financing of the CPR extension in the east. The government, however, could ill afford the collapse of the CPR, financially or politically. Rather than let it go under, the government intervened during the 1884 session and provided a loan of $22.5 million to the company for four years. Tupper was hurriedly called back from London, where he now was Canada's high commissioner, to steer the railway loan through the Commons.

But the CPR's financial difficulties persisted. The CPR and Van Horne were throwing everything into the project, with the intention of completing the line years ahead of the deadline – but the construction costs were enormous, with upwards of 35,000 men on the payroll, and the expenses of 1884 brought the CPR once more to the brink of financial collapse. It was touch and go all during the spring of 1885.

At this juncture an ostensibly unrelated episode intervened to determine the future of the national undertaking. The second Métis uprising in 1885 provided the railway with an opportunity to demonstrate its importance to the country's security. Van Horne undertook to move troops west from Montreal to Fort Qu'Appelle in eleven days. In less than a week the first troops arrived in Winnipeg by train, and a few days later troops were marching north from the CPR line to the Saskatchewan River (Fleming's son

Franky was one of those soldiers). The CPR's ability to move more than three thousand troops to the Prairies quickly enabled the government to put down the rebellion before it got out of hand. That fact was not lost on a grateful Parliament, and in July a relief bill was passed assuring the necessary loans to complete the railway line.

Fleming was elected to the CPR board of directors in 1885. This was a curious twist of fate, considering the way he had previously been shunted aside by the government. Stephen wrote to Fleming upon his appointment:

> I can assure you I am greatly pleased at having you for a col-
> league in the Direction of the CPR. Without expecting you
> to incur any responsibility in respect of what has been done
> in the past, we shall all of us best fulfill the duties attaching
> to the position by looking to the future rather than to the
> past, and each doing what we can to promote the services of
> the enterprise.[9]

The construction of passages through the Rockies and Selkirks was a near-impossible challenge for the work crews. The maximum gradient allowed on the CPR was 2.2 percent, or 35 metres per 1.6 kilometres, and Rogers had worked out a way down the Kicking Horse River that did not exceed this; but as construction neared, serious obstacles became apparent. The stability and safety of some of the roadbed was doubtful and would require boring a tunnel 1,423 metres long, through solid rock, with conse-quent further delay in completing the line. Fleming suggested that the CPR instead seek permission to build a temporary, much steeper line. The govern-ment agreed and the end result was a 6.4-kilometre stretch with a gradient of 4.4 percent and then, after a relatively level interval, a second descent almost as steep and long. Four locomotives were required to haul even the shortest freight train up the gradients.

The CPR line was almost complete by late 1885, an incredible five years ahead of schedule. Only a small section of track to connect the eastern and western sections remained to be laid. The regular train for Winnipeg left Montreal on 27 October, with a private car at the rear, in which sat three CPR directors – Donald Smith, William Van Horne, and George Harris. A fourth director, Sandford Fleming, joined the train at Ottawa. After a two-day delay in Winnipeg, the train became a "special" and steamed westward. Fleming rode on the rear platform for part of the way, watching for familiar landmarks from his trek with Grant and Sandford Jr. two years before. The train reached Revelstoke, at the western crossing of the Columbia River, fifty-six hours after leaving Winnipeg; the line ahead was not yet complete.

By nine in the morning on 7 November 1885 the last rail was laid in place at Craigellachie (so named by Van Horne for the meeting place in Scotland of the Clan Grant, to which George Stephen and Donald Smith were related), 45.5 kilometres west of Revelstoke. All that remained was for the last spike to be driven home; the honour fell to Donald Smith as the most senior director present. Fleming later recalled the scene:

> It was felt by all to be the moment of triumph. The central figure – the only one at the moment in action was more than the representative of the railway company, his presence recalled memories of the Mackenzies, Frasers, Finlaysons, McLeods, MacGillivarys, Stuarts, McTavishes and McLoughlins who in past generations penetrated the surrounding mountains. Today he is the chief representative of a vast trading organization in the third century of its existence. The spike driven home, the silence for a moment or two remained unbroken. It seemed as if the act now performed had worked a spell on all present and each was abandoned in his own thoughts. The silence was however of short duration. The pent up feelings found vent in a spontaneous cheer the echoes of which will long be remembered at Craigellachie.[10]

A few minutes later the train passed over the newly laid rail amid further cheering, and made its way to Port Moody and the Pacific on 8 November. It was five years and eighteen days since the contract had been signed with the CPR Company – a phenomenal achievement by Van Horne and his work crews. Some final work to reinforce the line had still to be completed, so the formal opening was delayed until the following spring. The first through train for the Pacific coast left Montreal on 28 June 1886, and covered the 4,640 kilometres in 140 hours.

The transcontinental railway was a reality. It had been achieved at enormous cost. The financial burden for the young country was staggering – the combined expenditure for the Intercolonial and CPR by the end of 1886 was $116.5 million. Thousands of men worked on the construction, many lives were lost, careers were broken, and governments toppled. But the costs could not detract from the monumental achievement of binding together a country east to west. Canada did not just happen, it was created by the vision, dedication, and sweat of men like Fleming and many thousands of engineers, labourers and politicians; it was a national undertaking, and it represented a commitment that was the country's greatest hope for its future.

CHAPTER 12

PACIFIC CABLE

Fleming's vision of a Canada united from one ocean to the other was bound up with his concept of a strong and united empire of British nations circling the globe. Building up Canada buttressed the framework of empire. The Canadian Pacific Railway would immeasurably increase the commerce of the British Empire, and improve the lines of communication between Britain and her far-flung dependencies. Canada's ties with Britain buttressed the young country's political independence in North America. At the same time, the Canadian government wanted to assert the country's autonomy.

There was nothing in Fleming's globe-straddling vision contrary to the growth of a strong and independent Canada. The whole of his labours on the Intercolonial and the CPR had been to that end. At the same time, however, he emphasized the benefits that could flow from a flourishing relationship between the nations of the British Empire. To his engineer's eye, modern and reliable communications were essential to the relationship. Empire-controlled transport and communications systems linking Britain first with Canada, and through Canada with Australia, New Zealand, India, and South Africa, it was believed, would be more secure than lines running eastward across alien and sometimes hostile lands in Europe and the Ottoman Empire.

Early in his railway engineering career, Fleming recognized the importance of the telegraph service to rapid communication; it was his practice to string telegraph lines ahead of the railway tracks he constructed across Canada. The first contract let on the CPR was for telegraph installations. The erection of telegraph lines ahead of the railway allowed the engineering branch in Ottawa to keep in constant touch with field operations. Fleming wrote to the superintendent of the Canadian Telegraph and Signal Service in June 1979 to broach the idea of a submarine telegraph cable extending beyond Canada across the Pacific Ocean.

> It appears to me to follow that, as a question of Imperial importance, the British possessions to the west of the Pacific

Ocean should be connected by submarine cable with the
Canadian line. Great Britain would then be brought into
direct communication with all her greatest colonies and
dependencies without passing through foreign countries.[1]

Fleming's final report on the CPR in 1880 dealt at length with the idea
of extending the CPR telegraph across the Pacific. He advanced several reasons in support of the idea: it would connect San Francisco, Chicago,
Toronto, New York, Montreal, Boston, and all the great business centres of
America direct with China and the principal Asian ports; it would open new
means of communication between America and Asia at much lower rates
than by existing channels, and unlike those existing channels it would not
pass through countries where different languages were spoken, thereby causing frequent transmission errors; it would complete the telegraphic circuit of
the globe, bringing Britain, Canada, India, Australia, New Zealand and
South Africa into an unbroken telegraphic communication with each other
that would be entirely independent of lines passing through foreign countries; and last but not least it would be under government control and so
immediately serviceable in any emergency. Fleming was too active by nature,
and too committed to Canada's development, to be sidelined by his dismissal
from the government's engineering branch.

Tupper knew this well, and in June 1880 saw to it that the government
proposed to the House of Commons that a company set up by Fleming
should be given exclusive privilege to land a submarine cable on Canada's
Pacific coast, and the right to string a wire for cable business on the Pacific
Railway telegraph posts. The submarine cable would run from Nanaimo to
the north of Vancouver Island, then to Japan, touching the Aleutian Islands
on the way. The proposal was debated in Parliament in March 1881; its most
important and certainly most controversial provision was a twenty-year
exclusive-privilege clause. In fact, there already was a potential spoiler for
Fleming in a separate application before Parliament from a British-based
company – the European, American and Canadian Cable Company – seeking to establish telegraph links between Canada, Britain, and "other countries," even though there was no mention of the Pacific.

The Liberals Mackenzie and Blake resisted granting Fleming a monopoly. The member for Victoria, Amor de Cosmos, already no friend of
Fleming over CPR affairs, had no sympathy whatsoever for Fleming's latest
scheme.

I look upon this Bill as simply a money-making Bill, like all
Bills of a similar nature. It is admitted by the Minister of

Public Works, that unless Mr. Fleming can get the exclusive privilege for twenty years he does not want to have anything to do with forming a company. To bring it right down to the point, it is simply this: Mr. Fleming or his associates believe they can make money by getting an exclusive right which they can sell in the markets of the United States, Great Britain or Europe, and they will be very handsomely paid indeed. I trust this House will follow the policy laid down by Her Majesty's Government in 1864–65, and deny to any company the exclusive right for twenty years, or longer or shorter period, of operating telegraph lines in any portion of this Dominion. The United States Constitution recognizes no such thing as a monopoly, nor does the constitution of any State recognize it. I can say, with respect to the line contemplated, what great advantage can Mr. Fleming and his associates gain, even in the money markets, except to make a sale of it at once?[2]

Fleming spent the next several days urgently looking into the background and intentions of the rival company, and reported to the public works minister that "I am advised that a submarine telegraph to Asia is entirely beyond the scope of the proposed company's powers, and that there is nothing whatever in the Bill to indicate that its promoters had or have the least intention of undertaking any works beyond the limits of the Atlantic."[3]

At the same time, he told the minister that, reasonable though his request was, he was prepared to drop the twenty-year monopoly provision. Fleming's proposal, thus amended, and the European, American and Canadian Cable Company plan, now expanded to include a Pacific cable, were both approved on 16 March.

Fleming despaired of ever raising the necessary financing without the monopoly clause, and with another company in the field. He was on the brink of scrapping the idea at the beginning of 1882, but the government encouraged him to persist. Fleming implored Sir John A. Macdonald to restrict the rival company to its original purpose, which was an Atlantic cable only. And in a last-ditch effort to keep the Pacific scheme alive, he asked the imperial authorities to consider a guarantee of assistance, in the form of either government telegraphic business or its equivalent as a subsidy in exchange for agreed rates for messages.

There were powerful forces at work, however, to ensure that Fleming's plan would fail. All telegraphic traffic from Britain to the eastern Empire travelled on commercial lines across Europe to Asia and Australasia. The two powerful London-based companies that controlled the field – the Eastern Telegraph, and the Eastern Extension Telegraph, both under the chairmanship of John Pender – were not about to yield their profitable advantage to a Canadian interloper. The managing director of the Anglo-American Cable Company wrote to Pender in 1880 to reassure him that the waters of the Pacific were much too deep to make a submarine cable possible, and that in any case the costs involved would be prohibitive.

These powerful interests succeeded in frustrating Fleming's scheme for three years, but Fleming refused to give up. He had concluded by now that a northern cable route to Japan was not necessary, and that a cable running direct from British Columbia to Australia was feasible; the line would pass from Vancouver to the Fiji Islands, touching the Sandwich Islands and Fanning Island, finally joining the existing Australian and New Zealand telegraph systems.

With the CPR telegraph line complete by 1885, Fleming wrote to the Canadian government in an attempt to revive the proposal. The Australian colonies had been linked to the United Kingdom by commercial cable since 1872, but charges were high and there was always the danger of interruption when political turmoil in Europe or Egypt assumed threatening proportions; Fleming contended that a Pacific route could transmit messages at less than half, and possibly as little as a third of present rates. Essential to the scheme, however, were government subsidies until the line became self-sustaining. According to Fleming, several governments, including Britain, Canada, Hawaii, Fiji, New Zealand, and the Australian colonies, were interested.

Advantage was taken of the Colonial and Indian Exhibition in London in May 1886 to convene a conference of all the governments concerned, to assess the prospects for a Pacific cable. Fleming travelled to London for the conference, leaving behind a great many commitments in Canada, including CPR and Hudson's Bay Company board meetings. Jeanie was in poor health and in no condition to travel; Fleming took his daughter Lily with him. Tupper was now Canada's high commissioner in London; the principals in Fleming's company – Randolph Want, Andrew Robertson, Matthew Gray, and Donald A. Smith – wrote to Tupper to demonstrate how the subsidies from the participating governments would end up at no net cost to them.

> As the Company would transmit all the messages of the various contributing Governments free, and the rates chargeable to the public for "through" messages would not be more than one-half the present regular tariff charges, Great Britain and the Colonies would save a much greater sum than the amount of subsidies proposed.[4]

The commercial companies were working to derail Fleming; Sir James Anderson of the Anglo-American Cable Company spoke of a plan by Pender that was at that moment being considered by the Australian colonies, guaranteeing to the Eastern Telegraph Company, its partners, and the Eastern Extension Company the average revenue derived from Australian traffic over the past three years. In return, the Australians could reduce user charges to whatever level they wished. The companies would gamble that the inevitable traffic increase would compensate for the low charges. The plan was tempting.

All the colonies and self-governments of the Empire assembled at a colonial conference in London in 1887 to commemorate the Golden Jubilee of Queen Victoria's reign. The colonial secretary, Sir Edward Stanhope, proposed that the agenda include consideration of postal and telegraphic communications. Canada's representatives included the Ontario lieutenant-governor, Sir Alexander Campbell, and Sandford Fleming. The delegates had two alternative communications proposals before them: Fleming's Pacific cable and Pender's rate reduction plan, both dependent on government subsidies or guarantees. When Fleming was called on to outline his proposal, Pender was asked to leave the room. Fleming told the delegates that without a Pacific cable, mercantile trade on the Pacific would be handicapped, and as for Pender's competing plan:

> I will only notice very briefly the letters of Mr. John Pender, which have also been placed in the hands of members of the Conference. Mr. Pender speaks on behalf of the existing Telegraph Companies, and it is not unnatural that he, and they, should be hostile to a new line which would undoubtedly destroy their monopoly and reduce the exceedingly high charges which they have so long enjoyed.[5]

Fleming rejected any suggestion by Pender that laying a submarine cable across the Pacific would be any more difficult than in the Atlantic, observing that the greater depth of the Pacific actually afforded an added element of security, since cables laid in shallow water, such as those of Pender's companies, were more exposed to the ravages of the sea, and so always in need of repair and replacement. Then there was the important question of rates: the ordinary charge per word from London to Vancouver was eight and a half pence; allowing for the long stretch across the Pacific would bring the rate to Australia to a total of one shilling, eight and a half pence. Pender's company was charging nine shillings fourpence.

Fleming addressed the matter of communications security:

> Mr. Pender urges that in case of war it would be impossible to
> protect cables laid across the Pacific. I venture to enquire,
> would it not be infinitely more difficult to protect the cables
> and the land lines of the Companies represented by the gentle-
> man? Look at the telegraph map of the world and judge of
> their respective security. The lines of the Eastern and Eastern
> Extension Companies have stations in two foreign countries –
> Egypt and Java – the one under the sovereignty of Turkey, the
> other of Holland. All, or nearly all, the cables of these
> Companies are laid in shallow water, and nothing could be
> easier than to drag them to the surface anywhere. From
> England to Egypt they skirt every country in Southern
> Europe, and are exposed at every point for the whole distance.[6]

As the conference progressed, a new proposal appeared for a Pacific cable,
submitted by a syndicate called the Pacific Telegraph Company; it was
known that Fleming had business connections with this new entrant, so
inevitably there were whispers that he was simply advancing his own interests. Fleming categorically denied all such suggestions:

> I wish it to be understood that I am not promoting any par-
> ticular company. I am here only representing Canada, and
> am endeavoring to promote to the best of my ability a work
> which I believe to be absolutely necessary for the security
> and prosperity of the British Empire. With regard to the
> company which has been referred to, I was opposed to being
> connected with it; I allowed my name to be used along with
> that of two other Canadian gentlemen as signatories, simply
> because we were strongly prevailed upon to do so, but I have
> now nothing to do with the company, and am not advocat-
> ing that company here at all today.[7]

In fact, by this stage Fleming preferred that the Pacific cable be undertaken
by governments rather than private enterprise, in the interest of efficiency,
security, and economy. He proposed one government-run and centrally
administered telegraph company, which would lay the Pacific cable, and seek
to buy out Pender's lines eastward to India, China, and Africa, so it would
become a globe-circling service. Fleming envisaged each of the participating
governments, except Canada, handing over its telegraph system to the central
authority – Fleming was not proposing, however, that the CPR, on whose
board he sat, surrender its lines.

The representatives of the competing telegraph proposals placed before the colonial conference were each given their day in court; Mr. Finch Halton made a pitch for his Pacific Telegraph Company, and Pender outlined his rate reduction deal, claiming it would reduce the current tariff by more than half. The conference wrestled with the competing schemes, with little idea of what direction it ought to be going in; in the end, it accepted the principle of a Pacific cable – a decision that was neither easily taken nor enthusiastically received by the authorities in London. The fact remained that Pender's companies already provided a service; there was little inclination to undertake huge new financial commitments to duplicate an existing service for an uncertain return and untested security. The conference delegates did, however, ask the British authorities to task the Admiralty to begin a survey of a possible Pacific route. London was distinctly cool to the idea, committing itself only to an incidental rather than a specific survey during the regular course of the Admiralty's duties in the Pacific. Fleming was enormously frustrated that the momentum he had built up with the Australian colonies should be thus dissipated by Britain's foot-dragging. In effect, the imperial government was telling Fleming there would be no real surveys until funding for a Pacific cable was assured, but funding was impossible without surveys to prove its feasibility.

The following year, the Canadian government seized the initiative and invited the colonial governments of Australia and New Zealand to send delegates to a meeting in Canada to consider telegraph and trade relations, and to arrange terms; later it was decided the meeting should be held in Australia, but in the end it was shelved in face of the proposed federation of the Australian colonies.

Fleming's wife, Jeanie, died in March 1888, only fifty-seven years old; her health had been delicate for several years. It was a cruel blow to Sandford who, in spite of his nearly constant travels, was a devoted family man. The children were grown up now. Frank, the oldest boy, was a cattle farmer at Weston; Walter was a military cadet at Royal Military College, Kingston; and Hugh had gone from Upper Canada College to medical school at Queen's College. The girls, Lily and Minnie, remained at home in Ottawa with their father. Only Bobby had followed in his father's footsteps to become an engineer and surveyor.

The Admiralty actually began soundings over the proposed Pacific cable route in 1888, but operations stopped without explanation in 1890. By coincidence or not, Pender's rate reduction scheme, which had dropped from sight after the 1887 colonial conference, surfaced again in 1890 as a specific proposal to the Australian colonies – user rates cut in half in exchange for a guaranteed return to Pender's company of an annual £54,000 subsidy.

Fleming was back in London with his son Hugh in 1890 to attend Hudson's Bay Company meetings, and to continue the assault on the Colonial Office, and on Pender. He wrote in considerable annoyance to the colonial secretary:

> Is the opinion of the Colonial Conference, unanimously expressed, to be unheeded? Is it expedient that Canada and the Canadian route should be wholly ignored? Is it desirable that any course should be followed which will debar the Canadian Dominion from co-operating with her sister colonies and with the mother country in a matter in which they have a common interest? I venture to think that aid in the way proposed to the existing companies would be fatal to any Pacific telegraph; it would be essentially a step backwards, and could lead to no permanent good, while the same outlay expended in another direction would result in incalculable advantages.[8]

When the imperial government eventually turned down Pender's scheme, the irrepressible Mr. Pender sought to plant a cuckoo's egg in Fleming's nest, arguing that should a Pacific cable be laid, it was for his company to do it; Pender reasoned that back-up facilities to secure communications in the event of disruption were essential, and only he could assure them. In an attempt to scare the government where it hurt most, Pender argued that an entirely separate Pacific cable undertaking would necessitate laying not one but two cables, at double Fleming's estimated £1.8 million; in other words, twice the annual subsidy from the colonies.

Fleming wrote to Pender, turning the arguments to his advantage:

> I am very glad to find you are coming to realize that it is absolutely necessary to have an alternative cable to Australia by way of Canada and the Pacific. I have always held and I now hold that the means taken to establish the new telegraph connection is entirely secondary provided that the new line is secured. Its establishment by whatever means is the primary consideration, and it is for the Governments concerned to decide how it is to be done. In my humble judgement if they consult economy and desire to secure cheap telegraphy, they will act wisely in making the work a public undertaking and in retaining it in their own hands under an efficient management.[9]

Fleming thought the idea of a second back-up cable was nonsense – disruptive earthquakes in the Pacific were rare and, in any event, one cable or two would be equally vulnerable to disruption. He observed that Pender's cables east of Aden broke down in May 1890, thereby isolating Australia, so that messages had to pass through Russia, Siberia, China, and French Cochin-China. This had opened the eyes of many Australians to the need for an alternative Pacific route, but unhappily for Fleming, still not quite enough of them. Pender's reduced rate plan was a surer thing than the much-talked-about but non-existent Pacific cable. Five of the Australian colonies – New South Wales, Victoria, South Australia, Tasmania, and Western Australia – signed on Pender's dotted line. Fleming's scheme was very much down, but not entirely out. It would not have been like him to surrender without a fight.

CHAPTER 13

THE ALL-RED LINE

The completion of the Canadian Pacific Railway led to a new awareness of the trade possibilities in the Pacific region, and with the 1887 colonial conference in London and a growing interest in closer imperial ties, Canadians became more mindful of the potential for increased commercial relations with Australasia. It was decided in 1889 that John Abbott and Adam Brown should visit Australia to meet with representatives of the colonies there, to consider the best means of developing trade. Macdonald wrote to Tupper on 14 August, "Abbott will be styled Chief Commissioner. I thought of joining S. Fleming on the commission, but it met with strong opposition in Council. Thompson says his evidence on the CPR arbitration is 'infamous'."[1]

In the event, various delays caused the mission to be postponed for years, but private initiatives to expand trade with Australia were taken. The Canadian Parliament in 1889 authorized an annual subsidy for a steamship service between Canada and Australia – the offer was taken up four years later by an Australian businessman, James Huddart – with the proviso that the service be operated on a monthly basis. The first steamer of the Canadian–Australian line left Sydney for Vancouver in May 1893. Huddart's three-year contract was eventually extended to ten years, to allow the service to become established on a firm footing.

John A. Macdonald died in 1891, and after a brief period with Senator Abbott as first minister, John Thompson became prime minister. With the Australian steamer service a proven success, the Thompson government resurrected the idea of a trade mission to Australia, and in September 1893 decided to send the trade and commerce minister, Mackenzie Bowell, to Sydney as soon as possible, to promote an extension of trade ties and to discuss the possibility of a telegraph line between the two countries. Not wanting to miss this unique opportunity to promote the Pacific cable plan, Fleming offered to accompany Bowell. Thompson put aside his misgivings about Fleming, which dated back to the Pictou Railway affair, and accepted his participation. Bowell and Fleming, with Fleming's daughter Minnie, set sail from Victoria for Sydney, Australia.

The ship arrived in Honolulu on 24 September and they met with the British minister there; the Hawaiian Islands were in a state of political unrest, but local businessmen were interested in promoting cable communications across the Pacific. Bowell invited the Hawaiian authorities to a conference proposed for the following year to discuss trade and cable communications.

Fleming had other reasons to be interested in the Hawaiian Islands. About 380 kilometres to the west was a tiny rock outcropping – Necker Island. Approximately halfway between Canada and Australia, it was the ideal situation for a telegraph-cable landing station. Necker had another thing in its favour – it was so desolate that there was no record of anyone ever having bothered to land there to claim it for any country, and sovereignty was important if a Pacific cable was to steer clear of foreign territory. Another, less attractive possibility was Fanning Island, which was annexed by Britain in 1888; but it was farther from the cable's starting-point in Canada. While he was in Honolulu Fleming drafted a memorandum recommending Necker Island as a landing station, and strongly urging Britain to lay claim to it. Bowell transmitted Fleming's note to the Canadian government, which in turn pressed the case on the imperial authorities.

In Sydney Fleming drafted a memorandum to all governments concerned, outlining in detail the Pacific cable proposal, but he was up against long odds; Pender had already sold his rates reduction scheme to five of the Australian colonies, which now were paying £53,400 per annum to Pender's company in return for a 50 percent reduction in user fees. To further complicate matters, the French had come up with a scheme of their own to lay a submarine cable from Queensland to the French penal colony of New Caledonia, and thence by stages to San Francisco. This plan threatened the commercial viability of the proposed Pacific cable.

Undaunted, Fleming proposed that the Australian colonies, New Zealand, Fiji, and Canada should be joint owners of the Pacific cable, which would be operated as a public undertaking. Most of the Australian governments were locked into paying the annual subsidy to Pender's Eastern Extension Company for several more years, but Fleming said the subsidy could be offset by the expected revenues from the Pacific cable, which would be shared by the governments.

Bowell and Fleming spoke to audiences across Australia, particularly chambers of commerce, on their twin themes of improved trade relations and closer communication links; the response varied from lukewarm to enthusiastic. The Brisbane *Courier* was among the believers:

> Mr. Bowell does not come alone. Himself on a semi-official visit for patriotic objects, he is accompanied by a veteran railway engineer of worldwide reputation, and who wears

the laurels deservedly won by a professional man who has superintended the carrying out of one of the greatest works of modern times – the Canadian Pacific Railway. Mr. Sandford Fleming has reached an advanced age [he was now 66 years old], but he is still imbued with the spirit of the victorious warrior, and would like to add to his achievements the promotion of an ocean cable uniting Australia with the Pacific slope of the Canadian Dominion, and binding these two great provinces of the British Empire with the mutually advantageous bonds of reciprocal trade. For whatever the benefit to be derived from a steamship service such as that which Mr. James Huddart has so pluckily started, that benefit will be insignificant by comparison with the advantage that would accrue from the direct communication between the two countries.[2]

But Pender's influence was everywhere; two days before Bowell and Fleming set out from Vancouver, the Colonial Office in London despatched two documents to the several Australian governments intended to show the impracticality of a Pacific cable – the one document from officials in the British Post Office, the other from the Admiralty's hydrographer. They raised all manner of objections, touching on cost, traffic, revenue, and technical problems. Fleming was furious. The Admiralty report was an old one, predating the 1887 colonial conference at which the principle of a Pacific cable had been endorsed, and it took no account of the surveys undertaken between 1888 and spring 1889. At the end of the Australian tour, Fleming sailed direct to England to set the record straight. Back in Ottawa, he reported to Bowell that the British papers were inaccurate and misleading. Fortunately, however, no great harm was done and a postal and telegraph conference of the Australian colonies at Wellington, New Zealand, in spring 1894 endorsed the Pacific cable project.

Bowell's Australian mission had been a triumph, imperial meddling notwithstanding, and it demonstrated that Canada was well equipped to mobilize international opinion when it was sure of its facts and the wisdom of the course it pursued. The Australian colonies agreed to send representatives to a conference in Ottawa in 1894 to encourage closer trade ties and discuss the laying of the Pacific cable. Fleming, meanwhile, was worried that if Britain did not stake a claim to Necker Island, another country would. It was apparent that Britain was in no hurry to do anything positive to promote the Pacific cable, and he concluded it was up to him to take drastic action.

Fleming wanted Necker under the Union Jack before the Ottawa conference, and in a move calculated to embarrass the British authorities out of their inaction, Fleming resolved to despatch his own one-man mission to the dismal rock, plant the British flag on it, and claim Necker Island for Britain. He entrusted the secret mission to a Toronto friend, a retired naval officer, R.E.H. Gardner-Buckner. Gardner-Buckner was instructed to catch the first available steamer leaving Vancouver for Honolulu; from there he was to charter a small boat to take him to Necker Island, and after making explorations and surveys of the two-kilometre-long rock, plant the British flag on it.

Two days after Gardner-Buckner set off, in May 1894, Fleming made the mistake of writing to Tupper in London informing him of the secret mission; Tupper confided in the Colonial Office, which reacted with fury. The British did not want to take any precipitate action in the area while Hawaii was in political turmoil. Fleming's envoy arrived in Honolulu to learn that the British government, quite unannounced, had hastily recognized Hawaii's sovereignty over Necker Island, before he could get there with his British flag, and had requested terms for British control over it for purposes of a cable landing station. The Hawaiians were as surprised as Fleming that they should be considered to own Necker, as no Hawaiian was known ever to have set foot on it. Rather than trust to luck or the British, however, the Hawaiians despatched a covert mission of their own, landing their minister of the interior on Necker to plant the Hawaiian flag. Necker Island thus was ruled out for a Pacific cable touching only on British soil.

Fearing what could result from the Ottawa conference, Pender wrote to the Colonial Office in April to register several objections to the proposed Pacific cable scheme. The existing telegraph service, he asserted, was established by private enterprise, and relied on little public assistance; a cable across the Pacific was unnecessary; to proceed with a Pacific cable would require an annual subsidy of £192,000; and it would do serious injury to the existing service and be unfair to his company. If, however, the governments were determined to proceed with a Pacific cable, Pender wanted the project for his own company.

The Ottawa conference was opened by the governor general, the Earl of Aberdeen, in the Senate Chamber in June 1894. All the Australian colonies except Western Australia and Fiji were present; so too was Hawaii. The delegates had a long agenda: adoption of the metric system, an imperial tariff union, improved postal services, and the Pacific cable. The New South Wales delegate introduced a resolution calling for immediate steps to provide telegraph communications between Canada and Australasia; he was as fed up with the British authorities as Fleming was:

> It is, I think rather unfortunate that the Imperial Government are not more energetic, if I may use such a term, in

carrying out their promise, because undoubtedly they made a promise to the effect that a vessel would be employed, and that the survey would gradually be completed, but instead of carrying on the survey which was commenced, the vessel was withdrawn, and so far as we know nothing further has been done.[3]

He was influenced, however, by Pender's plea for special consideration.

If the construction of the Pacific cable means the destruction of the other cable, I do not see that by constructing the Pacific cable and destroying the other we shall be in any better position than we are at present ... We feel that there is work for both these cables, and that we should assist in every possible way we can in doubling this communication between the parts of the Empire concerned.[4]

Fleming launched a vigorous attack on Pender.

There are many leading minds in the mother country, in Canada and throughout the colonies who recognize the value to the Empire of a telegraph across the Pacific, who indeed wonder that it has not before now been established. One reason is the opposition of a strong joint stock company, the managers of which have exercised their hostile influence in every possible way since the first inception of the project.[5]

Pender's purpose was primarily to protect the interests of his companies' shareholders; while Fleming took a larger view, and a longer one: appealing to sentiments favouring closer imperial ties, secure communications in time of war, and increased trade between Canada and Australia. Time was not on his side, however; others were becoming interested in the commercial possibilities of a Pacific cable, notably the French and the Americans.

Fleming told the delegates:

With respect generally to the opinions expressed by Sir John Pender – it is not possible to set out of view that as chairman of a prosperous company desirous of avoiding competition, he is interested in the non-completion of a telegraph across the Pacific. Such a line of telegraph would lead to a revolution in the status of the enterprise he directs, and one of the first results would be a reduction of profits. It may, however, be pointed out that a line across the Pacific must be accepted as a fact of the near future, whatever rivalry it may create. The progress and well-being of Canada, Australia and the Empire, cannot be retarded in order that the lucrative business of a private company may remain without change. Even if the chairman of the Eastern Extension Company succeeded in converting us to his commercial ethics, that the profits of the monopoly he represents must be maintained inviolate, it does not follow that the project of a Pacific cable would not be carried out in some form, even if Canada and Australia abandon it. There are indeed unmistakable signs that a Pacific cable may shortly be carried out by France and the United States. We all know that France has already completed a section of 800 miles [1,280 km] at the southern end, and the United States has recently expended $25,000 in making an elaborate survey of about one-third the whole distance running southward from San Francisco. With a rival line in foreign hands, it is easy to see that the Eastern Extension Company would gain nothing while the Empire would lose much.[6]

Fleming expanded the delegates' horizons with a proposal that once the Pacific cable was built it be extended from Australia to India and South Africa and on to England, completing the circuit of the globe, an "All Red Line" touching on British soil only – those large splashes of British imperial red on world maps of the nineteenth century, on which the sun never set.

Opinion at the Ottawa conference was running strongly in Fleming's favour; the Queensland representative declared: "We have decided to oppose, as much as it was in our power to do, what we have regarded as a grasping monopoly – the Eastern Extension Telegraph Company."[7] Perhaps the greatest impetus, however, came from the threat of the French and the Americans getting the jump on them; the conference concluded that immediate steps should be taken to provide a Pacific cable free from foreign control, and urged that the imperial government be asked to proceed quickly with a survey whose expense would be borne equally by Britain, Canada, and the Australian colonies. The conference also proposed that London take immediate steps to secure a neutral landing ground on one of the Hawaiian Islands, so that the cable would remain under exclusive British control, and that the cable be extended from Australia to the Cape of Good Hope.

A month later, advertisements appeared in the London *Times, Canadian Gazette, Electrical Review,* and *British Australian* calling for proposals from cable contractors in three different forms: the cable to be owned and controlled by government, by a subsidized company, or by a company under a government guarantee. The rates between Britain and Australasia were to be three shillings a word for ordinary messages, two shillings for government telegrams and one and a half shillings for press messages. Offers were invited on eight different routes via Fanning, Necker, or Honolulu. Four tenders were submitted, all at under Fleming's estimated £1.8 million. The very fact that companies were prepared to bid put to rest Pender's question of practicality. It also showed that the project could be executed entirely on British soil, that there was no need to wait for preliminary surveys, and that it could be done within original cost estimates.

Still the British dragged their feet. The government in London had only a slim majority, and no heart to press forward with an undertaking of such magnitude. After the election in 1895, however, the new government of Lord Salisbury had a big majority, and the colonial secretary, Joseph Chamberlain, was a champion of closer imperial ties. Chamberlain was quick to grasp the significance of a Pacific cable for imperial unity, and he set the British government on a new and more positive course; in July 1896 he set up an imperial committee to consider the idea, including on it two representatives each from Britain, Canada, and Australia. The Canadian commissioners were Lord Strathcona (Donald A. Smith), who now was Canada's high commissioner in London, and Alfred G. Jones of Halifax. Fleming was asked by Canada's new prime minister, Wilfrid Laurier, to join the Canadian delegates as an expert adviser.

The committee met from July to October, and in its report of January 1897 concluded that while the Pacific cable was practicable, a preliminary survey was essential. The route should run from Vancouver Island, by way of Fanning or Palmyra Island, Fiji, and Norfolk Island, with branches from there to Queensland and New Zealand. It was recommended that ownership be by the governments concerned, with management in the hands of a manager in London supported by a small board representing the various governments. Ten years after the 1887 colonial conference, progress on the Pacific cable had slowed to a snail's pace. Fleming's path had been strewn with apathy, suspicion, and outright hostility. He was undaunted, however, and wrote to Laurier in May 1897 to report that, "there are the strongest reasons for taking a hopeful view of the proposed Pacific Cable."[8]

Fleming saw Laurier off for London in June 1897 for the Diamond Jubilee Colonial Conference, at which the Pacific Cable Committee report was high on the agenda. Matters were complicated, however, by yet another proposition from the Eastern Extension Company and consideration was deferred. Pender was trying now to short-circuit the Pacific cable by proposing a cable of his own, running in the opposite direction, from England to South Africa, Mauritius, and Western Australia, also touching only on British territory. Pender's proposal was highly interesting to the Australian colonies, but it cut Canada completely out of the picture; an irate Fleming complained to Laurier that

> in the interests of the Eastern Extension Company the Pacific cable has been declared to be impracticable; its cost has been greatly exaggerated; it has been denounced as a work which could not be maintained without burdensome subsidies; it has been stigmatized as inimical to telegraphy and trade; and it has been decried and misrepresented in every possible manner. The explanation is to be found in the fact that the company is unwilling to relinquish its monopoly and to rest satisfied in the future with a reasonable return for capital invested.[9]

The imperial government wanted the Australian colonies to take the lead on a Pacific cable, but so long as they remained politically disunited their hands were tied. The Australasian colonies convened a postal and telegraph conference in Tasmania in March 1899 to consider how to proceed; they agreed to reject Pender's latest scheme and repeated the call for a Pacific cable. While things were looking up again for Fleming, it was too soon to relax. He wrote to Chamberlain in October 1898 to float his new idea for the extension of the Pacific cable to a worldwide, state-owned imperial telegraph system, stretching from Vancouver to Australia and New Zealand, across the Indian Ocean to South Africa, and then across the Atlantic to the eastern shore of Canada.

> Such a system of cables would complete the telegraphic circuit of the globe, and would constitute a base for connecting every one of Her Majesty's possessions and naval coaling stations (Gibraltar and Malta excepted) by the most perfect means of conveying intelligence at our disposal. Moreover, the connection would be formed by a system of all-British deep-sea cables in the position where they would be least vulnerable.[10]

It was apparent by the spring of 1899 that the Pacific cable battle had been won; in April the Colonial Office wrote to the Canadian high commissioner and the agents general for the Australasian colonies with proposals for proceeding with it. Final agreement was reached in July at a meeting in London between Chamberlain, the chancellor of the exchequer, Sir Michael Hicks-Beach, and the agents general for New Zealand, Victoria, Queensland and New South Wales (the representatives of Western Australia and South Australia were absent, both colonies securely in Pender's fold).

The Eastern Extension Company might have been more successful in its efforts to torpedo the Pacific cable if it had not clung to its old bad habit of asking for government subsidies; belatedly, Pender and his associates realized their folly and set about to play their trump card. First, though, they would make one more appeal to the government's sense of fair play.

In June 1899 a deputation from the Eastern Telegraph Company and the Eastern Extension Company, led by Lord Tweeddale and John Pender, called on Chamberlain and Hicks-Beach to state their views on the all-British Pacific cable. Not surprisingly, Tweeddale and Pender objected to what they considered unjust state interference and competition in an area traditionally served by private enterprise. They argued that their proposed Cape route was superior from the commercial, strategic, and financial points of view. If, however, the government was determined to press on with a Pacific cable, common justice dictated that the Eastern Extension Company be given the job. Chamberlain and Hicks-Beach were singularly unimpressed by Tweeddale's bold assertion that his companies had operated largely independent of government support. The chancellor cautioned Tweeddale: "You had better not press the argument of subsidies too far; it may be against yourselves. You have had £1 million of public money."[11] Nor did Tweeddale's plea of unfair competition sit well; Hicks-Beach did not mince words:

> To speak very plainly, you put forward a contention which to my mind, is in no way justifiable. You have received your-selves very considerable subsidies from the Australian Governments, and you are asking at the present time for a subsidy for an all-British cable between this country and the Cape of Good Hope. I confess that in these circumstances for you to come here and tell us that we have no right to aid in the establishment of a cable between Canada and Australasia because you hold the monopoly of the existing telegraphic communication between England and Australia is saying too much – more than the House of Commons would grant.[12]

It was now or never for the Eastern Company to play its final suit, although Pender did not live to deal it. The company would drop its request for subsidies altogether, and it would not insist on a guarantee against competition. All that it asked in exchange for a Cape-to-Australia line was the right to lease a land line across Australia, and to open offices in Australian cities so it could deliver and collect its messages. The user rate would be reduced to four shillings per word from the outset, with further reductions on a sliding scale as business increased. Attractive as the offer was, it was too late. Several governments were even now ratifying the Pacific cable agreement.

The Canadian Parliament agreed in June 1899 to the terms of the Pacific cable undertaking, as worked out in London – the project would be managed by an eight-man board of commissioners representing the participating governments, and costs would be apportioned with Britain bearing five-eighteenths, Canada the same, and New Zealand, Queensland, New South Wales and Victoria two-eighteenths each.

Speaking to the resolution in the House of Commons, Tupper heaped praise on Fleming for his enormous contribution to the scheme. As for the Eastern Company, Tupper said:

> It would be almost impossible to over-rate the enormous influence which the Eastern Extension Telegraph Company, then represented by the late Sir John Pender as its president, was able to exercise in England. Its ramifications, its long arms, seemed to reach everybody. The Post Office Department, the Admiralty Department, the Colonial Office, in fact, all the departments, seemed to be, more or less, under the potent influence which that company was able to bring to bear.[13]

The Canadian authorities were concerned about the potential spoiler effect of the Eastern Extension Company's latest offer, just when victory seemed assured. Laurier sent a wire to the Australians in January 1900: "Would sincerely hope that project of Eastern Extension Telegraph Company will not be accepted. Any kind of delay at this moment might be fatal."[14]

In the end the potential damage of the competing Cape-to-Australia line was minimized, with only New South Wales succumbing to an agreement with the Eastern Extension Company. The Pacific cable agreement was intact and the contract was awarded on 31 December 1900, one day before the birth of the Australian Commonwealth. The route would run from Vancouver Island to Fanning Island, Fiji (Suva), Norfolk Island (Sydney Bay), with separate lines to Queensland and New Zealand.

A quarter century had passed since Fleming first promoted the concept of a Pacific cable. The inaugural message was sent over the line on

31 October 1902 – a greeting from King Edward VII to the people of Fiji. The first message received in Canada was a message of congratulations to Fleming from New Zealand's premier. On opening day Fleming sent two telegrams addressed to the Canadian governor general – one in a westward direction around the globe, the other eastward; if Pender had still been alive he would have chortled at the thought that Fleming's messages were carried part of the way on eastern cables.

The Pacific cable was a success from the outset, and its financial situation improved with each passing year, allowing the participating governments to decrease their subsidies. The line was seriously under-utilized, however, sitting idle for twenty out of every twenty-four hours for want of traffic. Fleming conceived a plan to promote its fuller use, which would also further consolidate the Empire; he wrote to the colonial secretary, the Earl of Elgin, in January 1906 to propose the establishment of a news wire service using the Pacific cable to disseminate news – an imperial intelligence service. The idea was not originally Fleming's; it was first introduced by Sir Frederick Pollock and Geoffrey Drege from the United Kingdom during a Canadian speaking tour in 1905.

Fleming envisaged a central intelligence board in London, with local boards in the capitals of the self-governing countries to collect, edit, and transmit information for simultaneous publication in newspapers all over the Empire. News would be carried free of charge over the Pacific cable during the quiet hours, at minimal extra cost to be borne out of profits. The Pacific Cable Board itself did not much like the idea because of the extra cost of manning the cable for longer periods. Fleming had an alternative plan, however, which would leave the question of the supply of news in the hands of the press, and lower the press rates on the cable to a nominal fee. The Ottawa board of trade, of which Fleming was a prominent member, became a leading promoter of the all-red line and the imperial intelligence service.

Fleming was not asked to participate in the 1907 colonial conference, possibly because he was too far out in front on the imperial federation movement, certainly beyond Laurier, but his views on a state-owned imperial cable circling the globe were put before the conference. With the self-governing members of the Empire growing more confident in their own nationhood, however, ardour for imperial union was waning and Fleming's federationist ideas lost their edge.

By now, Fleming was a grand old man, the friend of statesmen throughout the British Empire, and an important voice on the benefits of closer imperial ties. Advancing years made scarcely a dent in his unrelenting travel, meetings, and speaking engagements. He crossed the Atlantic in both directions sometimes twice a year, and travelled between Ottawa and Montreal for board meetings of the CPR and Hudson's Bay Company. There always were requests outstanding for him to address an audience; tributes came his way from all directions – honorary degrees from St. Andrews University, Columbia, and his own Queen's University. He was elected a Fellow of the Royal Society of Canada, the Royal Geographical Society, the Geological Society, the Royal Historical Society, and the Victoria Institute.

Grandchildren and great-grandchildren filled Winterholme in Ottawa. There were many visitors; on his seventy-fifth birthday Signor Marconi, the inventor of wireless telegraphy, lunched with Fleming. He recorded his seventy-eighth birthday in 1905 in his diary: "After dinner had a splendid game of chess with Sandford H., Walter and Hugh, with three separate boards. We played over an hour and I had the good fortune to win each of the three games."[15] Fleming travelled frequently to Weston, to visit his son Frank and his family at the farm. There were occasional trips on the train to Halifax, but less often now.

CHAPTER 14

CEMENTING THE FOUNDATIONS

While the railway and the Pacific cable enterprises went forward, Fleming had also been deeply involved with the evolution of Queen's University in Kingston. His friend George Grant was appointed principal of Queen's College in 1877, two years after he became moderator of the Church of Scotland. Almost immediately, Grant launched a drive to raise $150,000 for new buildings and more spacious grounds. The foundations were laid in 1879, and the completed main building opened in 1880. Fleming responded generously to Grant's appeal, and took a lively interest in the college he had first seen in 1845.

Queen's College was created in response to the creation of King's College, Toronto, in 1827, although King's only opened its doors in 1843. Until King's was secularized in 1849 to become the University of Toronto, it was the preserve of the Anglican Church in Upper Canada. For ten years, beginning in 1829, the Presbyterian Church had made futile attempts to have the constitution of King's broadened; the Presbyterian synod then decided to establish a college of its own and set about to raise funds, chiefly among Scottish settlers; an appeal was launched in October 1839.

Kingston was chosen as the site for the new college, and it was named Queen's for the new monarch who had recently ascended the throne. A royal charter was granted in 1841, and Queen's College at Kingston opened its doors in a clapboard frame house in March 1842 with two professors and about twelve students. For the first ten years the college expanded, but then fell on hard times in the 1860s. The Presbyterian Church relinquished control of Queen's in 1875, thus placing a greater onus on the college to support itself. Grant's appointment as principal in 1877 promised to breathe new life into the college. One of his first aims was to secure it on a sounder financial footing.

Three years after Grant's appointment, Queen's was required to elect a new chancellor; three names were put forward – Prof. Goldwin Smith, Vice-Chancellor Blake and Sandford Fleming. While Grant stoutly denied any influence in the matter, he was doubtless implicated in advancing his friend's cause. The candidacy was an unusual one to say the least, considering that Fleming had no university training and indeed, had finished his formal schooling at the age of fourteen. Fleming was embarrassed by his apparent lack of qualifications, but Grant was at pains to reassure him.

> I have great faith in the ability of the Graduates to discern between quiet and spread-eagle merit, and I think that both of your competitors savour somewhat of the latter. It is not a knowledge of Latin and Greek that makes a man learned. If a man can think, he is learned. A knowledge of grammatically constructed languages, rich with stores of thought, helps a man to think. But the coming in contact with nature and the world on a large scale, if he have the seeing eye and honest heart to begin with, are still better helps.[1]

Grant was so confident in Fleming's election that a few days later he sent suggestions for his inaugural address, even though the results would not be known for some months.

Word came through by mail from a jubilant Grant in March 1880.

> Hurrah! Three times three. The voting papers have just been opened, and you are elected Chancellor of Queen's University. Blake ran you close. You led only by four votes. The lawyers of course went for him, and the strong Temperance Men. (P.S. When men vote without being asked, and when each voter has to pay $1.00 in order to have his vote made valid, an election means something – Hooray!)[2]

The City of Kingston presented the new main building (first called the Arts Building, now Theological Hall) to the university on 14 October, and Fleming was installed as chancellor shortly thereafter; he made oblique reference to himself and his deeply felt lack of a university education in his address to the graduates.

> The education of men who have distinguished themselves in any way without university training has been laboriously and in most cases imperfectly obtained through private study; and as exercise invariably strengthens the faculties whether physical or mental, the very obstacles which they have overcome have been of service to them in obtaining any degree of cultivation that they may have reached. But if you ask such men, they will tell you that their path to

success would have been infinitely easier, and that they
would in all probability have occupied a much larger sphere
of usefulness to mankind, if circumstances had favoured
them as they are now favouring you.[3]

Fleming regarded his appointment as more than honorary, and kept in
close touch with Queen's affairs, attending convocations and executive meetings. He always stayed, while in Kingston, with the Grants. George Grant
kept up a running correspondence with Fleming about college matters.

The Ontario premier, Oliver Mowat, offered in 1883 to make Grant
provincial minister of education, but he declined, preferring to continue his
work at Queen's. In 1885 the province invited Queen's to surrender its charter and become part of the provincial university. Everyone connected with
Queen's was unanimous in their determination to maintain its independence;
without provincial support, however, the university had to find new sources
of revenue to keep afloat.

Grant had his eye on the pocketbooks of the Montreal philanthropists –
Sir Hugh Allan (whom Fleming had approached in 1878 during an earlier
appeal and from whom he had got $5,000), Sir George Stephen, and Donald
Smith. Grant asked Fleming to approach Stephen and solicit a $50,000 or
$100,000 contribution. The Queen's Jubilee Endowment Fund was so
named in honour of Queen Victoria's jubilee coronation anniversary year;
Grant had not overlooked the fact that Smith and Stephen intended to give a
million dollars to build and endow a hospital in Montreal to commemorate
the Queen's Jubilee; one-tenth this amount for Queen's College was nothing
to them. A Queen's Endowment Association was established, with Fleming as
its president, and branches organized all over Ontario; Fleming and Grant
travelled to their meetings to boost the subscription drive – by December
1887 there was $220,000 in the fund.

Fleming made other important contributions to Queen's; the idea of the
Queen's Quarterly publication was his, conceived on the basis that something
more substantial than the students' *Journal* was needed. He took enormous
satisfaction in his re-election time and again to the university's highest office;
he served as its chancellor for thirty years until his death in 1915. Fleming
was separated from a dear friend when George Grant died in 1902 after a
lengthy illness. The students had decided in November 1901 to raise funds
for a new convocation hall to be erected in his honour. Grant did not live to
be present when Fleming laid the cornerstone for the new building in
December 1902; Grant Memorial Hall was completed and formally opened
in November 1904. It still stands today, as does Fleming Hall, the engineering building.

Fleming saw Prime Minister Wilfrid Laurier and his party off for England in June 1897. They were on their way to attend the Diamond Jubilee Colonial Conference, and although Fleming was not part of the Canadian delegation this time, he was not forgotten in London: a telegram arrived at Winterholme from the governor general advising that the Queen had bestowed on him the order of Knight Commander of St. Michael and St. George. Henceforth he would be known as Sir Sandford Fleming. A number of friends, notably George Grant, had promoted Fleming for a knighthood.

Sir John A. Macdonald died in 1891. The Conservatives continued in power through four short-lived administrations, including that of Charles Tupper, until the 1896 federal election brought the Liberals, under Wilfrid Laurier, back from the political wilderness. Laurier's ascendancy coincided with a new wave of economic activity and optimism in Canada. After a drop in immigration in the last years of the nineteenth century, new waves had begun pouring in from Europe to the Prairies. New strains of early-maturing and frost-resistant wheat encouraged bumper harvests for export. The Canadian Pacific Railway still had an effective monopoly over western rail traffic, but that control now was being contested.

William Mackenzie and Donald Mann, who had worked on the building of the CPR, in 1896 bought the rights to the troubled Lake Manitoba Railway and Canal Company, which had not gone anywhere since its inception in 1889. Mackenzie and Mann laid 136 kilometres of track in the first year, taking the line to Winnipegosis. In 1899 the company was renamed the Canadian Northern Railway; it expanded rapidly as Mackenzie and Mann bought up small lines and built new ones. By the end of 1903 the Canadian Northern Railway had 2,730 kilometres of track, a fifth of which was in eastern Canada. By 1905 they had a main line from Winnipeg to Edmonton, and from Winnipeg to Port Arthur, with some lines east of Lake Superior including access to Montreal. By about 1903 Mackenzie and Mann had in mind to put together a transcontinental railway that would rival the CPR.

At the same time, the Grand Trunk Railway was growing in a big way; by the turn of the century it had about 8,000 kilometres of line in eastern Canada. Its new general manager, Charles Melville Hayes (who drowned in the *Titanic* sinking several years later), was determined to break out of the east and make something more of the GTR. Laurier knew well the benefits that could flow from a national railway project – Sir John A. had demonstrated *that* – the sense of national purpose, the economic development, not to mention the political credit. There were apparent advantages to a second transcontinental line; with the west filling with immigrants and spreading farther and farther north from the CPR line, it was becoming a problem to move the vastly increased grain harvest. Northern Ontario was a neglected wilderness of barely cultivated farmland, abundant stands of timber and pulpwood, and enormous mineral and hydroelectric potential. Northern Quebec, too, was overlooked as immigrants arriving in Montreal caught the first train west. A railway line west from Quebec City through northern Quebec and northern Ontario, passing south of James Bay and north of Lake Winnipeg, then across the Peace River district to Port Simpson on the Pacific coast, would respond to all these problems, giving breadth as well as length to the country. Quebec City could become a port to rival Montreal, and Port Simpson to rival Vancouver.

Laurier was in favour, but at the same time mindful of the political pitfalls in such an ambitious scheme; he was determined to make haste slowly. During the winter of 1902–1903 the government tried but failed to bring the GTR and the CNOR together, with the GTR providing service in eastern Canada and the CNOR covering the west. Mackenzie and Mann did not want to share the action, nor was Hayes much interested. Accordingly, Laurier signed a contract in July 1903 to go it alone with the Grand Trunk. The government undertook to build a national transcontinental railway from Moncton to Quebec City, and westward via North Bay to Winnipeg, which would then be leased to a subsidiary of the GTR. The Grand Trunk Pacific Railway Company would in turn build a new railway line across the Prairies and through the Yellowhead Pass to Port Simpson. The line would run a total of 5,669 kilometres from coast to coast, and the cost of construction would be enormous; Laurier's railway minister, Andrew George Blair, resigned over the issue, but the bill passed, nevertheless, in September 1903.

So now there were two new transcontinental lines destined for the Pacific, both to run via the Yellowhead Pass – which Fleming had first promoted thirty years before. The country was deeply divided, however, over whether a second transcontinental line was needed or affordable. The Montreal *Star* was among those opposed: "We should not waste any money on that mad route, unknown, unsurveyed and uninhabited, through the north country, over granite ranges from Winnipeg to Quebec."[4]

Despite his advanced age, Fleming kept up an active pace; now seventy-seven years old, yet still full of ideas and enthusiasm, he went to Toronto in February 1904 for a number of speaking engagements. He addressed the Canadian Club on the subject of railways in an address he called "Build-Up Canada." His words showed that his vision of the future was as clear and far-reaching in old age as it had been in his youth. Forty-six years had passed since Fleming spoke to a gathering in the Port Hope Town Hall about his dream of a railway spanning the continent; harking back to the origins of the Canadian Pacific Railway, Fleming told his Canadian Club audience:

Precisely as we have today, there were men then, who inscribed on their banners the words "build-up Canada," and visionary and impracticable as it seemed to many, they formed the resolution to carry their standard across the home of the buffalo and the distant Rocky Mountains ... There is a wide interval of time between then and now. During the forty-five years which have passed, many hands and many minds have been actively engaged in building up Canada. One and all have done their part; each in his own sphere has helped to advance our country and shape its history. An occasional retrospective glance such as I have indulged in, is not undesirable for many reasons, but we must never forget to look forward. The advancement of the Dominion should be, and is, the first consideration with every true Canadian. To build up Canada and give her a prominent place among the nations is our legitimate ambition, and we must see that the elements of national strength are steadily kept in view. If much has been accomplished, much also remains to be done, and we must all endeavour to see that it is well and wisely done.[5]

The great challenge that lay immediately ahead, he said, was the building of a new transcontinental railway along the northern route. The single thread of CPR track was not sufficient to sustain the economy or guarantee the security of Canada, and if the unity of the Dominion was left insecure, the integrity of the Empire was imperilled. Fleming called attention to the vast, empty region north of Lake Superior, unserved by any railway, and about which little was known. The agricultural, mineral, forest, and hydroelectric potential of the region was enormous, but until now had been ignored. Fleming pointed to a large-scale map of Canada on which he had marked, in bold letters, Quebec City, Norway House (at the north end of Lake Winnipeg), and Port Simpson. The three centres were in a nearly straight line, and represented the shortest route from ocean to ocean. He urged the earliest possible start on construction, at least for the portion from Quebec to the Prairies, and advanced several reasons to commend a northern railway. The country, he said, should avoid concentrating the whole traffic of the Prairies along one line near the international boundary. The larger spaces of the Prairies north of the CPR line remained to be opened up; a railway on the northern route would be the shortest line between the Atlantic and Pacific, and the most direct for the harvest of the northern Prairies. A northern line devoid of gradients would also be a cheaper means of transport than a line that carried the harvest to the Great Lakes for trans-shipment on lake freighters. It would be more secure, and it would broaden the Dominion by converting a wilderness into an active and thriving part of the country.

Fleming trusted to the high-mindedness of the people of Montreal, Toronto, and Winnipeg to accept the virtues of a northern route that would bypass their communities. He concluded:

> Our aim is to make the Dominion compact, strong and prosperous. Our design is to have one Canada from the St. Lawrence to the mountains. Under the free institutions which we have inherited from the Motherland, with a virile population which has sprung from the foremost European races, united in this favoured land by common interests and common sentiments, we look forward to our destiny without fear and with much hope. We desire to make our country a great northern nation, in family affinity with an Empire whose noblest aspiration is peace and good will to all the nations of the earth. This is the high ideal we set before us in our strenuous efforts to build up Canada.[6]

Laurier turned the first sod on the National Transcontinental Railway (NTR) at Fort William in September 1905, and the affiliated Grand Trunk Pacific Railway (GTPR) began construction at Portage la Prairie the following year. As many as twenty-five thousand men worked on the construction at its peak. Henry Cambie wrote to Fleming from his home in Vancouver in December 1909:

> There is any amount of railway excitement here – the Grand Trunk Pacific and the Canadian Northern are continually discovering new routes and new passes – which the public believe, and are amused at for a short time. But so far they have all been routes reported on in detail by some of your assistants thirty-five years ago ... This is the most astonishing town! – increasing by 10,000 people every year – all of whom bring money – mostly from Saskatchewan and Alberta. Everyone is prosperous! – any number of houses building – but they can't be run up quickly enough! They are sold before they are half built – I have sold what little property I had, and am afraid to purchase more – surely these excessive values cannot last![7]

The first train from Winnipeg to Prince Rupert via the Yellowhead Pass arrived in April 1914. The NTR came into operation a year later. Mackenzie and Mann also chose the Yellowhead Pass for their Canadian Northern Railway (CNOR), which then followed Fleming's route down the Fraser River to Vancouver. In 1908 the CNOR laid a line north of Lake Superior from Toronto to Sudbury, then through the northern Ontario wilderness to Port Arthur. Freight service between Toronto and Winnipeg began in spring 1915; by September the line was open from coast to coast. While the GTPR-NTR line had direct government participation, the CNOR also did well by the government with large land and cash grants, and enormous bond issue guarantees. Over time the CNOR and GTPR were merged with government railways, including the Intercolonial, to form the Canadian National Railways (CNR) by the end of January 1923. Although Fleming died some years before, he lived long enough to see the realization of his dream of a transcontinental train that ran through the Yellowhead Pass.

The Canadian Institute Fleming helped found in Toronto in 1849 had gone from strength to strength over the decades. It had actively promoted both the universal standard time movement and the Pacific cable, and it was still, in the 1890s, one of Fleming's preferred sounding boards. In December 1892 he presented a paper on the subject of postage stamps; nearly fifty years after he designed Canada's first adhesive postage stamp, Fleming brought to the public's attention certain postage design faults that had been perpetuated since the beginning. The three-penny stamp of 1851 had a small figure 3 at each of its four corners, to denote the value, and the practice of using small, coloured corner numbers had been followed ever since, yet colours were no help to the colour-blind (including Fleming). The design fault, then, rested in the fact that the stamp's value was not shown with sufficient clarity. Fleming proposed that the Queen's head be retained on postage stamps, but only occupy the upper half of the stamp, leaving sufficient space in the lower portion for a single large figure to denote the value. Alternatively, he suggested, the Queen's head could be replaced by an imperial crown surmounting a shield on which would be inscribed a single large numerical figure denoting the stamp's value.

The governor general, Lord Minto, attended the fiftieth annual meeting of the Canadian Institute in December 1899; in its first year membership numbered 64, five years later it was 508; by 1899 the institute had established itself as one of the country's most important professional associations.

Fleming was often invited to give expert advice to business and industry. He was asked by the Ottawa Committee of Lumber Manufacturers in 1888 to examine the Ottawa River between Grenville and Ottawa, to see to what extent refuse from the several sawmills interfered with public and private rights along the river, and more especially, to determine to what extent navigation was obstructed. The problem was examined in general by Fleming, and in detail by Sandford Jr. under his father's instructions. They submitted their report in January 1889. While there was no doubt that the aesthetic quality of the river was marred by the large patches of sawdust and wood shavings on its surface, Fleming could find little evidence of any serious problems, except for certain private landholders along the river on whose property the effluent washed ashore. In fact, many people along the river scooped up sawdust from the water and dried it for winter fuel. Fleming's soundings of the river showed no evidence that the flow of water was interfered with to any appreciable extent, except directly in front of the Rideau Canal in Ottawa where there was a deposit of sawdust that could be cleared by dredging.

Church and business affairs also took much of Fleming's time in his later years. When George Grant became moderator of the Presbyterian Church in 1899, Fleming was appointed secretary of a committee to draft a new prayer book, "Aids for Social Worship." He attended board meetings of the CPR and Hudson's Bay Company in Montreal until he stepped down in 1907. In 1906 he was elected the first honorary president of the newly formed Alpine Club of Canada, a successor to the club he and Grant had started in Rogers Pass in 1883.

Among Fleming's many business interests, he was president of two cement companies: the International Portland Cement Company in Hull, Quebec, and the Western Canada Cement and Coal Company in Exshaw, Alberta, which he, his son Hugh, and J.S. Irvin founded. The Hull company was a profitable concern, but the Exshaw venture lost money from the start. Hugh Fleming oversaw the construction and start-up of the Exshaw plant from the Banff Springs Hotel, travelling each morning by train to the work site an hour away. There were construction delays, and the plant was a year late coming into operation in 1908. Even then, things went badly for the Exshaw venture; strikes by railway employees in late 1908 and coal miners in 1909 hit the company hard. The start-up problems were compounded by the commercial depression of 1908 and the fall in cement prices. The company's creditors, notably the Bank of Montreal, were crowding in, but the best the company's directors could do was to borrow more money to meet the interest due on bonds, and to arrange with creditors to carry their claims until business improved.

There was a ray of hope, however, for the beleaguered Exshaw company. Max Aitken (later Lord Beaverbrook), a thirty-year-old capitalist on the rise, was asked by the Bank of Montreal to look into the affairs of three cement companies in which it had invested. Aitken saw an opportunity to bring off the biggest business merger to date in Canadian industrial history. The demand for cement now exceeded supply, and the industry was protected by a substantial tariff. Aitken secured control of some of the key companies, and then revealed his merger plan. His Canada Cement Company was formed in September 1909, and by November it held options on thirteen companies, including those in which Fleming had an interest.

The board of directors of the Western Canada Cement Company at Exshaw recommended to its bond- and shareholders in October that they seize the chance to transfer controlling interest to the Canada Cement Company.

> Having in view the difficulties under which the Western Canada Cement Company was labouring, your Directors felt that in order to preserve the business of the Company for its bondholders and shareholders it would be highly desirable to join with the other companies in the establishment of a new consolidated company (now known as the Canada Cement Company Ltd. with an authorized capital of $30 million). To have remained aloof and endeavoured to compete with such a powerful organization as the Canada Cement Company would in your Directors' judgement have been suicidal and, having regard to the crippled condition of this Company's finances, might have culminated in a short time in the sale of the Company's assets at the suit of its bondholders and their almost certain acquisition by the Canada Cement Company or its friends at that Company's own price. Consequently your Directors entered into negotiations with the promoters of the Canada Cement Company for the purchase by it of the Western Cement Company's assets. After prolonged negotiations with the view to making a bargain as advantageous as possible for the bondholders and shareholders of your Company, your Directors reached terms with the Bond and Share Company (the negotiators) not, it is true, in all respects as they would wish, but the best possible that could be obtained.[8]

A.J.P. Taylor, in his biography of Beaverbrook, said of the proposed sale of Exshaw that, "Fleming, the experienced old financier, perhaps himself now the cat's paw of others, was proposing to take the young financier Aitken for a ride."[9] It is not at all clear, however, which one was in the driver's seat. The Exshaw company was debt-ridden, but it was only a small part of a big merger deal. According to the Exshaw shareholders' notice, an offer had been made for the company in spite of its desperate financial situation. The bidder, the Bond and Share Company, was a holding company of which Aitken was chairman.

Fleming was invited to become honorary president of Aitken's Canada Cement Company; according to Taylor, Aitken was making use of Fleming's name to facilitate the floating of the merger. Fleming, in turn, purchased a stake in the new company. The Canada Cement Company Charter named three people as provisional directors – Senator W.C. Edwards, Senator Robert Mackay, and William Maxwell Aitken.

Before very long the deal to take over the Exshaw company began to unravel. The Canada Cement Company board agreed to take all the cement companies, except Fleming's Exshaw operation. According to Taylor, Aitken had done what he set out to do: "he had used Fleming's prestige and had not been gulled over Exshaw."[10] Hugh Fleming wrote to his father on 10 February 1910:

> Several members of the Board of Directors of the Canada Cement Company have expressed their disapproval of the manner in which that Company was being conducted. It is claimed that the affairs of the Company are not known to the Directors; that the Board has not met for over two months, and that there are rumours afloat that are injurious to the Company. I understand there is a desire to bring certain matters fully before the Board at its next meeting on Thursday next at 11am and as the Exshaw affair is to come before the Board on that day it may be well for the Exshaw Company and for the Canada Cement Company too if all members of integrity and honour should be present ... I don't think it is necessary that you should attempt to explain our own [Exshaw] situation to them except to the effect that there seemed to be no doubt that the affairs of the Canada Cement Company were being influenced by individuals who had no relation to its business affairs but who were actuated only by their own personal interests, and that these influences were endeavouring to bring about a breach of faith with the Exshaw Company.[11]

The Board eventually did agree to take over the Exshaw Company, but at a price lower than that proposed in the option, and offered Fleming $50,000 if he would sign a letter accepting the deal. Canada Cement had now secured Exshaw along with Fleming. Fleming later repudiated the Exshaw deal.

At the 10 March meeting of the Canada Cement Company Board, Fleming refused to approve the company's financial statement. The first line of the statement caught Fleming's eye because it appeared incorrect based on his knowledge of the value of the properties acquired. The purchase price was $14,629,000, but securities to the value of $27,228,000 were handed over to Aitken's Bond and Share Company as the negotiator of the deals. Fleming considered the over-issue of securities a misappropriation, and urged Canada Cement to negotiate with the Bond and Share Company for the return of the over-issued portion of securities, or otherwise account for the profit it made in the transaction. Taylor said that Aitken's relatively small share of the overall profit, "seemed much larger to the financially-innocent who did not appreciate, as many people still do not, that the value of a share is what a buyer will pay for it and not the nominal sum inscribed on its face."[12] In this case, the buyer, Canada Cement, was also the vendor, Bond and Share Company, to the extent that Aitken was common to both.

Fleming was concerned not only with the propriety of the transaction but also with the effect it could have of raising the price of cement to the public. The Canada Cement Company solicitors advised that an action could not be sufficiently maintained against the Bond and Share Company. A legal adviser to Aitken called on Fleming in an effort to dissuade him from pressing further for an investigation.

Fleming resigned his seat on the Canada Cement Board in February 1911, and that spring wrote to the prime minister, Wilfrid Laurier, to ask that in the public interest an investigation be launched under the authority of the government. Laurier invited Fleming to his office a week later to discuss the matter, and subsequently the minister of labour sent Fleming a letter, at Laurier's request, enclosing a copy of the Act to Provide for the Investigation of Combines, Monopolies, Trusts and Mergers, along with forms for procedure under that measure. The dispute with the Cement Company was exposed to public view when articles appeared in the newspapers. The federal election intervened and Laurier was swept aside by Robert Borden and the Conservatives. Fleming wrote to the new prime minister in October to renew his appeal for an inquiry, by royal commission or otherwise.

> In this land of schools and colleges, of YMCA and other associations, in this land of churches of every kind, in this young nation with its business integrity and fair name in the process of making, are we to regard the plan of "getting rich quick" exemplified in this instance, as the highest ideal to be

placed before the youth of Canada to follow? We may indeed
find men learned in law who are ready to advise that the
transaction alluded to is "legal and binding", but if this
transaction, or any transaction be inconsistent with the
terms of "the Decalogue", if its tendency be to degrade public morals, surely a parliament representing the Christian
community of Canada should have little difficulty and no
hesitation in removing the inconsistency. Obviously the rule
ought to be of universal application, and in the formation of
companies in the future, over capitalization should be rigid-
ly restricted.[13]

Borden replied a month later. First, the rights of the Canada Cement
Company shareholders, as well as the rights of the respective companies
whose assets were transferred, were not properly the subject of investigation
by a royal commission but rather, could be argued in the courts. Second, as
far as the public interest demanded an investigation of such matters, the government expected soon to establish a permanent tariff commission with powers of inquiry.

In the event, there never was an inquiry, nor did the matter go before the
courts; as for the ill-starred Western Cement Company at Exshaw, the
Canada Cement Company bought up the mortgage debentures, but since the
interest on them was in arrears, the company foreclosed and took it over. In
an out-of-court settlement, Fleming paid $75,000 to the Bank of Montreal
in part payment of the interest outstanding on Exshaw; the bank wrote off a
portion of its claims, and Aitken put up $20,000 on condition that Fleming
withdraw his charges. A.J.P. Taylor called it "Danegeld": "When Fleming was
totally defeated, Beaverbrook contributed $20,000 to help him out, solely
out of softheartedness." After all the bad blood, it is hard to imagine Aitken
feeling softhearted toward Fleming.

Who was hoodwinked, Aitken or Fleming? Aitken contended that with
the Exshaw plant he was being asked to saddle Canada Cement investors
with the liability of an unproductive and overpriced concern.

It was certainly far easier to be pliable than to be firm. Every
kind of private pressure was brought to bear on me to accede
to the purchase of the property. When this failed, all the
immense engines for the formation of public opinion which
were at the disposal of the opposing forces were directed
against me in the form of vulgar abuse. And that attack was
very cleverly directed. It made no mention of my refusal to

buy a certain mill for the combine at an excessive cost to the shareholding public. On the contrary, those who had failed to induce me to break faith with the investing public appealed to that public to condemn me for forming a trust. I am prepared now to confess that I was bitterly hurt and injured by the injustice of these attacks. But I regret nothing.[14]

But was Aitken as steadfast as he suggested, once confronted with the Exshaw fiasco? According to Taylor:

> The storm fell on Aitken. He had promoted the merger and taken the credit for it. Now he got all the blame. Jones and the Cement Board were unruffled. They challenged Fleming to appeal to the courts. He did not take up the challenge. Aitken suggested yielding over Exshaw, or as he put it, "buying off the Norsemen".[15]

Beaverbrook's biographers are divided in their views of Aitken's handling of the Cement Company merger; F.A. Mackenzie is satisfied Aitken was in the clear:

> The young financier won out and time has since afforded the best justification of his policy ... To this day there are many people who, when Beaverbrook's name is mentioned, whisper the word 'cement'. Did they fully know the facts they would realize that the cement trouble was proof of Max Aitken's financial soundness, if proof was needed.[16]

Alan Wood is not so sure:

> On the available evidence we can only return a verdict, in this particular case, of 'Not Guilty' or 'Not Proven'. We can only say that Aitken made his money in his cement as in his other deals, by the usual capitalist method of selling things for more than he paid for them, and that in the process he evidently outsmarted others in Montreal. It also seems plain that the margin of profit was so huge that a vast fortune could be made without necessarily going beyond accepted standards of business behaviour: on this I know no absolute proof, either way.[17]

Aitken's business acumen cannot be faulted. Why he made an offer for Fleming's Exshaw Company, which was so clearly in trouble, and later withdrew it, inevitably remains a matter of speculation. Was it a device to win Fleming over in the interest of assuring the Bank of Montreal's backing for his larger merger plan? After all, Fleming's CPR friends had close ties to the Bank of Montreal.

In August 1908 Fleming put a proposal to the executive of the Halifax Canadian Club – it was widely known that 2 October of that year marked the 150th anniversary of responsible government in Nova Scotia, and the first responsible government in Britain's overseas possessions. A tablet commemorating that fact would be unveiled at the provincial legislature in August. Fleming suggested it would be fitting to do something on a bigger scale, more visible, to serve as a constant reminder to future generations of the democratic process put in motion in 1758. He proposed the erection of a memorial tower. Little more than a year old, the Canadian Club was handed a great challenge, spurred on by the promise from Fleming of land for a park on the Northwest Arm of Halifax, provided it did its part. The proposal gathered momentum and on 2 October, the 150th anniversary date, the foundation stone for a memorial tower was laid by the lieutenant-governor on a forty-hectare park site on the Northwest Arm donated by Fleming, in pouring rain, with the guests huddled under a canvas awning.

A competition was held for the design of the tower, and the winning architect's plans were unveiled in October 1910. The tower was to be 33 metres high, 9 metres square at the base, and in the style of an Italian campanile. The completed tower was dedicated by the governor general, the Duke of Connaught, in August 1912.

At the age of eighty Fleming decided to set down in writing the story of his long and varied life, but only as he wanted to be remembered; a place in history was important to him. But the prospect of sifting through a lifetime of papers was too much now. He had been a hoarder and a saver of souvenirs all his life; he wrote copiously, and in turn received a heavy mail, most of which he preserved. Fleming had also kept up an uninterrupted diary since he was a teenager, although the entries became more infrequent and summary over the years. The library at Winterholme was crammed with Intercolonial and CPR reports, pamphlets and studies on universal standard time and the Pacific cable, Canadian Institute proceedings, and papers from the many scientific associations of which he was a member. There were company reports from the Hudson's Bay Company, the CPR and the cement companies, accounts, thick letter books of official correspondence spanning the decades of his life on the railways, and convocation addresses from

Queen's. In 1907, Fleming turned to a young friend, Lawrence J. Burpee, the Ottawa librarian and historian, to write his biography.

Burpee took on the assignment, but the project dragged on interminably, because the work was constantly interrupted: the biographer's problem was that he had to moonlight to make ends meet, and so took on all manner of more immediate literary assignments. He wrote to Fleming in December 1911 to suggest that the royalties on the proposed book, likely to be $500 or more, be advanced to him to provide the wherewithal to get on. Fleming sent Burpee a cheque by return mail, but for $50, not $500. The book project continued at a snail's pace; Burpee dropped into Winterholme whenever he could, to gather up another sheaf of diaries or letter books, and to leave rough drafts of chapters for Fleming's approval.

Fleming was not looking for an unvarnished biography. The old man had never got over the wrongs he felt had been done to him by the politicians, the press, and some of his recalcitrant and rebellious CPR staff. This was his last, deliberate attempt to exorcise the ghosts that haunted him, and threatened his place in history, and so most of the controversy and criticism in Fleming's life were assiduously cut out. Missing altogether from the Burpee biography, for example, is the royal commission on CPR affairs; there is no mention of the damaging disputes with Marcus Smith, Horetzky, and Moberly. The book was a whitewash; it was published finally in fall 1915, eight years after it was begun. Fleming never saw it in print; he died in Halifax on 15 July. His work was done and, so he thought, his place in history secured. But his contemporaries knew better; it would take more than the Burpee biography.

Fleming's triumphs and his travails can only be properly understood in the context of his times. In the ferment of the emerging Canadian federation, everything was in the making: political parties, the economy, a coalescing national identity. The players in this large drama were often acting in the dark; the rules of the game were being made up as they went along. This was open territory for power-brokers and financial wheeler-dealers; alliances were rapidly formed, and shifted just as quickly. Broken alliances could and did lead to suspicion, and to back-stabbing. It was an age of strong convictions – many held deeply to the promise of Confederation, but others did not, or at the least were sceptical; some harboured a vision of a Canada extending from the Atlantic coast to the Pacific, but others believed, just as deeply, that the scarce resources of the young country should be concentrated on consolidating rather than too rapidly extending the 1867 base. The country had embarked on projects of gargantuan proportions by any measure, physical or economic, starting from a pitifully small human and financial resource base.

The stakes were high, with political and financial fortunes to be made or broken, and the future of communities, regions, and businesses hanging on the pace and location of railway building. It was inevitable in these circumstances that political skullduggery and financial chicanery should run riot. To stand still in face of the dynamics at work was to fall behind.

Fleming was no exception in playing fast and loose. He was a visionary and a talented engineer, gifted with a terrier-like perseverance. He was politically astute but not overtly partisan; yet, rather than saving his skin, his aloofness from party politics was his ultimate undoing. A resurgent Conservative Party used him as a whipping boy to get at the opposition Liberals in advance of a federal election. Their main prey was not Fleming; some Conservatives were driven by personal ambition to hobble the heir apparent, Tupper, and all were out to tear down the Liberals. Fleming gave his enemies plenty of ammunition; he did not administer the engineering department well, always doing better in the field than in the office. He was absent too much, albeit through no fault of his own, for his health suffered from driving himself too hard on the Intercolonial surveys, then taking on the added, and colossal, burden of the CPR survey at the same time – it was too much for one person's shoulders to bear.

In all likelihood Fleming did line his own pockets on the Pictou Railway construction, and for that he stood condemned by many in Nova Scotia and in Canada for years to come. He was too close to Tupper for comfort, with their joint business ventures, and Tupper's award to him of the Pictou construction contract in a secret and quite possibly illegal way. It suggested pretty strongly a conflict of interest, if not worse.

The Canadian foundations were laid by such people; there was nothing unique, in the circumstances of the time, in the way Fleming went about his business. What was more special was the breadth of his vision, and the tenacity with which he pursued his dreams for his adopted country; Fleming was one of the earliest to envision one Canada, from Atlantic to Pacific, and then to commit his prodigious talents and energy to its realization.

A Note on Sources

The principal published sources of material consulted in the preparation of this work are listed in the bibliography that follows. Of these the most important are the published works of Sandford Fleming himself including his important history of the Intercolonial Railway, *The Intercolonial: An Historical Sketch of the Inception, Location, Construction and Completion of the Line,* and the travel commentary, *England and Canada – A Summer Tour between Old and New Westminster.* Fleming's several published papers and reports to Parliament on railway affairs are also essential reference material.

Manuscript and other sources consulted are indicated in the endnotes, and of these the principal was the large collection of Fleming Papers in the National Archives of Canada.

NOTES

Chapter 1: Old and New Worlds

1. Hutchison House Museum Archives, Peterborough Historical Society.
2. Ibid.

Chapter 3: Intercolonial Beginnings

1. "A Letter from Leonard Tilley on the Intercolonial Railway, 1863," *Canadian Historical Review,* vol. 45 (Toronto: University of Toronto Press, 1964), 125–29.
2. Nova Scotia House of Assembly, *Debates and Proceedings,* 1866.
3. Journals of the Nova Scotia House of Assembly, 1867, Appendix No. 21.
4. National Archives of Canada (hereafter NA), Macdonald Papers, 125178, 30 July 1889.

Chapter 4: The First National Undertaking

1. Sir Joseph Pope, ed., *Correspondence of Sir John Macdonald* (Toronto: Oxford University Press, 1921), 14.
2. NA, Fleming Papers, vol. 57, 195.
3. NA, Macdonald Papers, 79570.
4. Ibid., 79553, 27 December 1869.
5. NA, Tupper Papers, 1348–50, 26 September 1869.

Chapter 5: Universal Time

1. *Proceedings of the Canadian Institute* (Toronto, July 1879).
2. NA, Fleming Papers, Consolidated Papers on Universal Standard Time.
3. Ibid.
4. Ibid.
5. Ibid.

Chapter 6: Looking West

1. *Proceedings and Transactions of the Royal Society of Canada 1889,* vol. 7 (Montreal: Dawson Bros. Publishers, 1890), 6.
2. *Correspondence of Sir John Macdonald,* 123–24.
3. Ibid., 124–25.
4. George M. Grant, *Ocean to Ocean* (Toronto: James Campbell & Son, 1873), 36–37.
5. Ibid., 48–49.
6. Ibid., 70.
7. Ibid., 265–66.

Chapter 7: Storm Clouds
1. Rt. Hon. Sir Richard Cartwright, *Reminiscences* (Toronto: William Briggs, 1912), 113.
2. NA, Fleming Papers, vol. 47.
3. *Journals of the House of Commons 1875,* vol. 9, Appendix No. 2, "Fifth Report of the Select Standing Committee on Public Accounts."
4. Ibid.
5. Ibid.
6. NA, Fleming Papers, vol. 47, 6 December 1877.

Chapter 8: Battle of the Routes
1. NA, Mackenzie Papers, 1604.
2. Ibid., 1607, 24 July 1877.
3. *Journals of the House of Commons 1877,* vol. 11, Appendix No. 2.
4. NA, Fleming Papers, vol. 7.
5. Ibid., vol. 47.
6. Ibid.
7. *Report of the Canadian Pacific Railway Royal Commission* (1882).

Chapter 9: Derailed
1. NA, Mackenzie Papers, Robson to Mackenzie, 26 September 1879.
2. J.W. Longley, *Sir Charles Tupper,* Makers of Canada series (Toronto: Oxford University Press, 1926), 179–80.
3. NA, Macdonald Papers, 111525, 25 October 1879.
4. Ibid., 11530, 2 November 1879.
5. Ibid.
6. NA, Smith Papers, 81, 12 January 1880.
7. Ibid., 82.
8. *Hansard,* 8 March 1880.
9. NA, Fleming Papers.
10. *Hansard,* 19 April 1880.
11. Ibid.
12. *Gazette* (Montreal), 6 January 1880.
13. Ibid., 7 January 1880.
14. NA, Fleming Papers, vol. 50, January 1880.
15. *Daily Globe* (Toronto), 28 January 1880.
16. Ibid.
17. NA, Fleming Papers, vol. 50.

Chapter 10: Witch Hunt
1. *Daily Globe* (Toronto), 28 June 1880.
2. *Report of the Canadian Pacific Railway Royal Commission* (1882).
3. Ibid.
4. Ibid.
5. Ibid.
6. Ibid.
7. Ibid.
8. Ibid.
9. Ibid.
10. NA, Fleming Papers, 16 April 1882.
11. "Letter to the Secretary of State, Canada, In reference to the Report of the Canadian Pacific Railway Royal Commission," *Sessional Papers* (No. 48) A, 1882.
12. Ibid.
13. NA, Fleming Papers, vol. 18.

Chapter 11: Finishing the Job
1. *Correspondence of Sir John Macdonald,* 274–75.
2. NA, Fleming Papers.
3. Ibid.
4. Sandford Fleming, *England and Canada – A Summer Tour between Old and New Westminster* (Montreal: Dawson Bros., 1884), 210–11.
5. Ibid.
6. Ibid., 266.
7. Ibid., 269–70.
8. Ibid., 271–72.
9. NA, Fleming Papers, 27 June 1885.
10. Ibid.

Chapter 12: Pacific Cable
1. NA, Fleming Papers, Consolidated Pacific Cable Papers.
2. *Hansard,* 1 March 1880.
3. NA, Fleming Papers, Consolidated Pacific Cable Papers.
4. Ibid.
5. Ibid.
6. Ibid.
7. Ibid.
8. Ibid.
9. Ibid.

Chapter 13: The All-Red Line
1. *Correspondence of Sir John Macdonald,* 454.
2. NA, Fleming Papers, Consolidated Pacific Cable Papers.
3. Ibid.
4. Ibid.
5. Ibid.
6. Ibid.
7. Ibid.
8. Ibid.
9. Ibid.
10. Ibid.
11. Ibid.
12. Ibid.
13. Ibid.
14. Ibid.
15. NA, Fleming Papers, Diary.

Chapter 14: Cementing the Foundations
1. NA, Fleming Papers, vol. 18.
2. Ibid.
3. *Queen's College Journal,* 1880.
4. *Star* (Montreal), 27 January 1904.
5. *Queen's Quarterly* 11 (April 1904): 404–17.

6. Ibid.
7. NA, Fleming Papers, Cambie Correspondence.
8. Ibid., vol. 15.
9. A.J.P. Taylor, *Beaverbrook* (London: Hamish Hamilton, 1972), 36.
10. Ibid., 37.
11. NA, Fleming Papers, vol. 15.
12. Taylor, *Beaverbrook,* 38.
13. NA, Fleming Papers, vol. 126.
14. Lord Beaverbrook, *Success* (London: Stanley Paul & Co., 1921).
15. Taylor, *Beaverbrook,* 64.
16. F.A. Mackenzie, *Lord Beaverbrook: An Authentic Biography* (London: Jarrolds, 1931), 43.
17. Alan Wood, *The True History of Lord Beaverbrook* (London: William Heinemann, 1965), 41.

BIBLIOGRAPHY

Bailey, Alfred G. "Railways and the Confederation Issue in New Brunswick, 1863–1865." *Canadian Historical Review,* December 1940.

Beaverbrook, Lord. *Success.* London: Stanley Paul & Co., 1921.

Berton, Pierre. *The National Dream.* Toronto: McClelland & Stewart, 1971.

———. *The Last Spike.* Toronto: McClelland & Stewart, 1971.

Burpee, Lawrence J. *Sandford Fleming – Empire Builder.* London: Oxford University Press, 1915.

Careless, J.M.S., ed. *Colonists and Canadians, 1766–1867.* Toronto: Macmillan, 1971.

Cartwright, Sir Richard. *Reminiscences.* Toronto: William Briggs, 1912.

Croft, Frank. "The Forgotten Whirlwind." *Maclean's,* 1 December 1954.

De Kiewiet, E.W., and Underhill, F.H., eds. *Dufferin–Carnarvon Correspondence 1874–1878.* Toronto: The Champlain Society, 1955.

Fidler, Vera. "Sir Sandford Fleming, Pioneer in World Communications." *Canadian Geographical Journal,* March 1963.

Fleming, Sandford. "Toronto Harbour: Its Formation and Preservation." *Canadian Journal,* 1853.

———. "Preservation and Improvement of Toronto Harbour." *Canadian Journal,* 1854.

———. *The Intercolonial: An Historical Sketch of the Inception, Location, Construction and Completion of the Line.* Montreal: Dawson Bros., 1876.

———. "Canada and Its Undeveloped Interior." *Proceedings of the Royal Colonial Institute,* 1878.

———. "Chancellor's Inaugural Address." *Queen's College Journal,* 1881.

———. *England and Canada – A Summer Tour between Old and New Westminster.* Montreal: Dawson Bros., 1884.

———. "Note on Postage Stamps." *Proceedings of the Canadian Institute,* December 1892.

———. "Postage Stamps and Colour Blindness." *Transactions of the Canadian Institute,* 1892.

———. "Canada and Ocean Highways." *Royal Canadian Institute,* 1896.

———. "The Pacific Cable." *Queen's Quarterly,* 1898.

———. "Early Days of the Canadian Institute." *Proceedings of the Canadian Institute,* 1899.

———. "The Meaning of the Pacific Cable." *Queen's Quarterly,* 1903.

———. "Build-Up Canada." *Queen's Quarterly,* 1904.

———. "Memories of the Mountains." *Canadian Affairs Journal,* 1907.

Glazebrook, G.P. de T. *A History of Transportation in Canada.* Toronto: Ryerson Press, 1938.

Grant, George M. *Ocean to Ocean.* Edmonton: M.G. Hurtig, 1967.

Kennedy, W.P.M., ed. "The Quebec Resolutions on Federation, 1864." *Statutes, Treaties and Documents of the Canadian Constitution 1713–1929.* Toronto: Oxford University Press, 1930.

Lamb, W. Kaye. *History of the Canadian Pacific Railway.* New York: Macmillan, 1977.

Lavallee, Omer. *Van Horne's Road.* Toronto: Railfare, 1974.

Legget, Robert F. *Railroads of Canada.* Vancouver: Douglas, David and Charles, 1973.

Long, Dorothy E.T. "The Elusive Mr. Ellice." *Canadian Historical Review,* March 1942.

Longley, J.W. *Sir Charles Tupper.* Toronto: Oxford University Press, 1926.

Mackenzie, F.A. *Lord Beaverbrook: An Authentic Biography.* London: Jarrolds, 1931.

Maclean, Hugh. *Man of Steel, The Story of Sir Sandford Fleming.* Toronto: Ryerson Press, 1969.

Maxwell, J.A. "Lord Dufferin and the Difficulties with British Columbia 1874–77." *Canadian Historical Review,* December 1931.

Ormsby, Margaret A. "Prime Minister Mackenzie, the Liberal Party, and the Bargain with British Columbia." *Canadian Historical Review,* June 1945.

Parkin, George R. *Sir John Macdonald.* Toronto: Oxford University Press, 1926.

Pope, Sir John. *Correspondence of Sir John Macdonald.* Toronto: Oxford University Press, 1921.

Preston, W.T.R. *The Life and Times of Lord Strathcona.* London: Eveleigh Nash, 1914.

Pryke, Kenneth G. *Nova Scotia and Confederation 1864–74.* Toronto: University of Toronto Press, 1979.

Roy, James A. *The Scot and Canada.* Toronto: McClelland & Stewart, 1947.

Saunders, E.M., ed. *The Life and Letters of the Rt. Hon. Sir Charles Tupper Bart. K.C.M.G.* Toronto: Cassell & Co., 1916.

Skelton, Oscar Douglas. *Life and Times of Sir Alexander Tilloch Galt.* Toronto: Oxford University Press, 1920.

Stevens, G.R. *Canadian National Railways.* Toronto: Clarke, Irwin, 1962.

Taylor, A.J.P. *Beaverbrook.* London: Hamish Hamilton, 1972.

Thompson, Dale C. *Alexander Mackenzie: Clear Grit.* Toronto: Macmillan, 1960.

Trotter, Reginald George. *Canadian Federation: Its Origins and Achievement. A Study in Nation Building.* New York: Russell & Russell, 1971.

Waite, P.B. "A Chapter in the History of the Intercolonial Railway 1864." *Canadian Historical Review,* December 1951.

———. *Canada 1874–1896: Arduous Destiny.* Toronto: McClelland & Stewart, 1971.

———. "Across the Rockies and the Selkirks with G.M. Grant in 1883." *Canada,* autumn 1973.

Wilson, Alan. "Fleming and Tupper: The Fall of the Siamese Twins, 1880." *Character and Circumstance: Essays in Honour of Donald Grant Creighton.* Edited by John S. Moir. Toronto: Macmillan, 1970.

Wood, Alan. *The True History of Lord Beaverbrook.* London: William Heinemann, 1965.

INDEX